PRAISE FOR *BOOKENDS*

"Zibby Owens's *Bookends* is a candid and charming memoir about the ups and downs of midlife through the lens of reading and books. Zibby, one of the most beloved book influencers in America, shares how books can help us through tough times. An inspiring and hopeful read."

—Arianna Huffington, founder and CEO, Thrive Global

"I knew Zibby was an ardent supporter of authors, but I didn't realize she was such a fantastic writer herself. Insightful, helpful, authentic, and unifying, the tone of this beautifully written, memorable memoir is just so Zibby. A great choice for every busy mom."

—Kristin Hannah, #1 *New York Times* bestselling author of
The Four Winds

"Zibby Owens has always been a terrific interviewer of authors, but it wasn't until I read her book that I realized how deep her passion for literature truly runs. Her story is a valentine to falling in love with the written word, and for a writer—and readers—that's the sweetest kind of tale."

—Mitch Albom, *New York Times* bestselling author of
The Stranger in the Lifeboat

"A tender, intelligent coming-of-age tale, by turns poignant and hilarious, *Bookends* gripped me from the first sentence. This is the kind of book you hide in the bathroom to finish, ignoring the cries of your kids and the ringing phone. But it's also a serious meditation on the dangerous constraints of contemporary motherhood and the nature of privilege. I dare you to read it and not fall in love with Zibby!"

—Joanna Rakoff, author of international bestselling memoir
My Salinger Year

"Zibby Owens has such an infectious enthusiasm—for life, for love, for her friends and family, but above all else *for books*—her prose glows with it. Thus *Bookends* acts on two levels: it is both a personal journey from mute child to gregarious author, who spends her days talking to and about writers, and a virtual bookshelf, the kind you sometimes find in a summer rental, groaning with well-loved spines."

—Deborah Copaken, *New York Times* bestselling author of *Ladyparts* and *Shutterbabe*

"*Bookends* is a testament to the healing power of literature, love, and above all, allegiance to one's true self. Zibby Owens guides us, like a comforting friend, through her journey of loss and reinvention, reminding us, in the end, of our endless capacity for love."

—Claire Bidwell Smith, author of *The Rules of Inheritance*

"Lucky for us, Zibby Owens—a relentless cheerleader for authors known and unknown—has paid homage to books and the role reading has played in her endlessly fascinating life by writing her own."

—Katie Couric, *New York Times* bestselling author of *Going There*

Bookends

Written by Zibby Owens

Princess Charming (illustrated by Holly Hatam)

Edited by Zibby Owens

Moms Don't Have Time to Have Kids: A Timeless Anthology

Moms Don't Have Time To: A Quarantine Anthology

Bookends

A Memoir of Love, Loss,
and Literature

Zibby Owens

Published by Little A, New York

www.apub.com

Amazon, the Amazon logo, and Little A are trademarks of Amazon.com, Inc., or its
affiliates.

ISBN-13: 9781542036993 (hardcover)
ISBN-10: 1542036992 (hardcover)

ISBN-13: 9781542036986 (paperback)
ISBN-10: 1542036984 (paperback)

Cover design by Zoe Norvell

Printed in the United States of America

First edition

To my entire family!
My four amazing kids.
My husband, Kyle.
My brother.
My parents, for fostering my love of reading from the start.
And to the janitor. You'll see what I mean.

Contents

AUTHOR'S NOTE

This memoir relies exclusively on my memory. I make no claim that the way I remember things is precisely how they occurred. I can't even remember where I left my phone two minutes ago. But I've done my best to recreate scenes, moments, and feelings to paint a picture of my story. If you know me and remember something differently, I apologize. You're probably right. But this is how my imperfect brain has stored life. So bear with me. Some names and identifying details have been changed to protect the privacy of individuals. Some entire portions of my life, like my first marriage and divorce, have been left out to protect my four children and our family. It's important to me that details about my kids and my family remain private.

B

1976–1994

One

LITTLE WOMEN

The first time I cried while reading was during *Charlotte's Web*. But it definitely wasn't the last.

I was eight years old and up past my bedtime. I snuck barefoot into the tiny bathroom I shared with my little brother to finish the last few pages. I hopped on the toilet seat lid and sat crisscross-applesauce while flipping through the book at my typical warp-speed reading pace.

Had you looked in from the outside of my fourth-floor Upper East Side apartment, you would've seen the dim flashlight dancing over the dark pages, a little girl in her cotton nightgown hunched over a book, motionless yet completely moved.

I could faintly hear my parents chatting in the other room, their voices muffled as I inhaled the ending. As Charlotte said goodbye to Wilbur, I burst into tears, my eyes so full and blurry I could barely keep reading.

I've been crying in bathrooms ever since.

That night, I was hooked. Yes, I was already a bookworm. My mother had been taking me to the library every summer since I was born, refilling her L.L.Bean tote bag with as many books as we could carry out. I couldn't wait to read through them, first her reading to me and then reading myself, so we could go back and wander through the aisles for more stories.

Every night, my mom would read to me before bed. First picture books, like *Tilly's Rescue* by Faith Jaques. Then *Little Women*, where I caught her trying to skip words. I read *Gone with the Wind* before I turned twelve. By high school, I'd read most of my mother's books, too.

My parents read constantly. Books lined the walls of our apartment and towered on both sides of their bed like the two lions outside the New York Public Library. That night in the mid-1980s, when I truly grasped the power of literature to evoke real emotion, changed my life. It sounds ridiculous, but Charlotte was my first experience with the sensation of loss. I grieved for her.

The cracking open of a book's spine has always been an exercise in self-discovery, healing, and fortification. That subtle whoosh when words spill out makes me salivate. Then the feel of the coarse pages under my fingertips delights my consciousness, the sudden sprinkling of syllables, the black-and-white letters in various patterns, coalescing to find their way directly to my heart. It's magic.

Sometimes I stroke the cover for a moment, that smooth wrapping paper giving hints of what's to come. I peek under the flaps like a child examining a birthday gift. I smell the pages and take my time getting deeper in. Title. Dedication. Previous works. And then, with a deep breath, I plunge into the first chapter like I'm flying off the white diving board into my black-bottomed childhood pool.

That underwater intimacy stays with me for decades and returns when I just glance at the book's spine, humbly lined up next to others on my shelf. It's no wonder that when I got out of bed after spending nine days with Covid, the first thing I did was pull every single book off the shelves in my home office. Over six hours, still weak and slightly dizzy, I touched every single book I owned as I reorganized my library into a rainbow of colored spines. Talismans. Stories. Reassurance. The characters greeting me, dancing around the dusty shelves, when I couldn't be with real people.

Books, for me, are lifesaving. They have been my companions, my teachers, my entertainment, my emotional outlets, my escape. They've taught me how to cook, how to love, how to mourn, how to cope, and how to feel. They've allowed me to sort through my own feelings and escape into someone else's.

I can recount exactly where I was when I read almost all the important books in my life.

Many books came at just the right time. In fact, some of them don't strike the same chord with me at this stage of life as they did originally. When I recently reread *Drinking: A Love Story* by Caroline Knapp, I wondered why I had so deeply related to it when it originally came out, although I still loved every page. On first reading, these books changed me. They are the vines I swung from to find my way through the jungle, one leading to the next until I found my way out.

Perhaps that's why I've now dedicated my life to becoming a book messenger, trying to deliver the right books to the right people at the right time through my podcasts, writing, publications, and book recommendations.

And I'm not alone. As I've connected with booklovers all over the world, I've found kindred spirits in so many others. My people. The friend in the group who is always recommending books. The one people call before they go on vacation for some up-to-date travel reading. The bookstagrammers. Publishing execs. Book reviewers. Fellow literary podcasters. There is a whole tribe of booklovers out there who sees their mission as helping others fall in love with books.

So here's my story, which includes many plot twists I never saw coming. Some good. Many tragic. Traumatic. All transformative. In dodging the roadblocks, I've ended up rediscovering my voice alongside the voices of so many others. And now I can't keep those voices inside.

———

If I were a child today, I would probably have been diagnosed with selective mutism and social anxiety. Back then, I was just "shy." I was the kid who would hang back at the beginning of birthday parties, clinging to her dad's leg. Once I felt comfortable enough, I was fine. My voice box could be unlocked and I'd act like myself again. I lost myself in books like *Are You There God? It's Me, Margaret* by Judy Blume and *The Secret Diary of Adrian Mole, Aged 13 3/4* by Sue Townsend. I knew I wasn't the only one with a strong interior monologue. Even throwbacks like *Marjorie Morningstar* by Herman Wouk took me out of my own insecurity and into someone else's life.

By seventh grade, it had gotten worse. Boys entered the picture on weekends and at interschool dances for my private all-girls' school. I'd get invited to the parties and then sit silently, typically smiling. I'd get asked to dance by the cute boys I had crushes on, but I wouldn't be able to say a word.

Some seventh- and eighth-grade boys would point it out.

"Who's your friend that doesn't talk?" they'd ask, snickering.

Each weekend was another test that I would fail. Another gathering where I'd wonder if I was literally invisible. I wasn't speaking, so no one spoke to me. I just sat there and listened. I analyzed conversation patterns. I tried to open my mouth but just couldn't. It wasn't that I didn't have thoughts; in fact, my thoughts were overflowing, pouring out of my brain like a receipt in an old-fashioned calculator, replete with the staccato melody of the keys and the whoosh of paper being spit out. I just couldn't get them from my head to my mouth and into the world.

So I wrote. I wrote all the time. I wrote in diaries, in school, in letters. I composed novels in my head and hastily transcribed them. On the page, I could always be me. Writing didn't scare me. It welcomed me with open arms and gave me an outlet for the ideas and comments fighting to come out of my brain. So I turned to it again and again.

My innermost feelings finally fled the confines of my forehead through my fingertips. It was a miracle. If only I could be like the characters in the Sweet Valley Twins books. If only I could escape into Judith Krantz's world in *Princess Daisy* instead of being stuck in middle school in Manhattan, silently slipping through packed sidewalks.

Back out in the world, surrounded by kids my own age, I was paralyzed. I felt distanced from my classmates and the guys we interacted with—their carefree ways, how they laughed and spoke so effortlessly. I wasn't like that.

———

When I was two weeks into ninth grade, my parents called me into their bedroom, just after Rosh Hashanah dinner. Almost as soon as our extended family had packed into the elevator to leave, my mom and dad told my brother and me that they were getting a divorce.

I was devastated; my dad and I had always been close. I couldn't bear the thought of not living with him. Of only living with my mom. My dad was so perfect in my eyes that I assumed she must've done something to scare him off.

My dad was the one I played thumb wars with while sitting on the cold wooden benches during High Holiday services. He was the one who sat on my bed when I was a little girl, telling me made-up adventure stories about a turtle named Murdle. He was the one who worked patiently with me while I tried to understand complex history texts like *The Communist Manifesto*. He was the one whose scribbled postcards I would receive at sleepaway camp ("I'm at Wimbledon!") and clutch to my chest.

His bright-blue eyes and pale skin that burned easily (and which, in the 1980s, he covered up with thick white zinc) complemented his black, wavy hair. He was handsome, athletic, and a high school basketball star even at five feet nine inches. His eyes and smile were always warm. Comforting. Twinkly.

He'd stroke my eyelids closed with his forefinger, one at a time, a move I've since stolen to help my kids sleep. Always armed with a clever pun, my dad would find the humor in any situation, making himself laugh. He amused us during dinner with the "napkin trick" and encouraged us to be members of the Clean Plate Club. When I felt excluded by friends in middle school, my mother would defer to him.

"He's so good at these types of things," she'd say, spritzing perfume on her deep olive skin while sitting at her skirted vanity, getting ready for a gala charity event.

My mother's blow-dryer was a part of our family. The scratchy, rounded brushes that she wielded to sculpt her super thick dark-brown hair always out on the dressing table. Her brown eyes focused on the mirror as she pumped those aerobics-toned, dancer-like upper arms to make herself into the dynamo she was. Petite. Constantly weight watching. Chain-smoking in between her half a grapefruit for breakfast and cottage cheese and fruit for lunch. My mother was the ultimate hostess, setting up the table for dinner parties days in advance with just the right tablecloths, candies, candles, and place cards.

She was also beyond thoughtful to me in her own way. She would leave me little love notes everywhere and pretend to be the "exam elf," with a tiny greeting waiting for me after each test.

Unfortunately, my parents fought constantly.

Knowing whom they've ended up with and who they've become now, it's a miracle to me that they ever got along. At age six, I was writing notes to them in the dark with my number two pencil, wearing my Snoopy nightshirt, and sliding them under their bedroom door.

"Mom and Dad, please stop fighting! I love you. Zibby."

When my dad would leave for one of his many business trips, his two-tone brown suitcase at the front door, I would cling to him.

"Don't go!"

"I'll be back before you know it, Zib," he'd say.

When he got back, he'd lift me up in a big hug and say, "I haven't seen you in a dog's age. Woof woof!"

Even, calm, thoughtful, and measured, my dad was consistent and loving. Even though he worked all the time, when he looked at me, I felt seen and appreciated, deeply loved. I always knew what I was getting. He never lost his temper or vented any business stress in my direction. His warmth was all I needed. Even administered in the smallest doses, his love could sustain me for days, like a vaccine that protects long after the needle has been discarded.

When my parents split up, I took out all my anger and aggression on my mother. I shouldn't have, but I was fourteen and that's how I handled it. She tried to defend herself by attempting to change my impression of my dad, to make him seem human, not superhuman, to point out his flaws so hers weren't the only ones I could see. It didn't work. Nothing anyone said or did could change the rosy glasses through which I saw him, and the more anyone tried, the more defensive I would get.

The night they told us about the divorce, I raced out of their bedroom into my own and threw myself on my heavily decorated canopy bed. I started calling my best friends to tell them what had happened, my brand-new cordless phone tucked under my right ear, feet up on the white painted desk that looked out onto Park Avenue. I was in a daze, a state of shock. How could I live without my dad? Every other weekend? That was nothing!

The next day, I came home from tennis practice to find all my dad's clothes on hanging racks in the lobby, slowly being loaded into cars. My nanny, Mary, a beautiful, plump woman from Alabama who had been with us since I was born and who had taken care of me like a mother, was crying as she wheeled out the plastic-wrapped suits. I walked over to her in my tennis skirt and polo, my ponytail bopping, and hugged her as tightly as possible, those smooth, thick arms of hers wrapped around me as they'd been for fourteen years. Our housekeeper, Connie, was running up and down, grabbing more belongings.

"Oh, Miss Zibber. I'm so sorry," Mary said.

I just cried.

"It's okay, Mary," I said. "It's okay."

When my dad came home from work, he met my brother and me at what used to be our house and walked us a few blocks down Park Avenue to the Lowell Hotel, where he'd taken a two-bedroom suite.

"Look, here's a room for you and Teds," he said, showing me the antique wooden double beds that my brother and I would share, the fancy drapes with a rope and tassel to hold them back.

"It's just temporary."

He stayed there almost four years.

To cope one afternoon back home after school, I took off my purple flats but kept on the matching outfit: a yellow-and-purple plaid skirt, purple tights, a yellow turtleneck, and a headband to boot. Then I turned on my shower. The water poured down in the late afternoon sun, the cars on Park Avenue inching downtown just outside my window, as I got into the shower. I sat down, fully clothed, drenched, and let the water drown out my day, my life, my feelings, until Mary finally came in and found me.

After that, my parents forced me to start seeing a therapist. Back then, medicating children wasn't a thing. Instead, I sank into the low velvety chair in the dark Upper East Side office each week, and confessed. As high school went on, I always had Dr. Klein's office to help me cope. When I started cutting myself in the privacy of my bathroom, taking a razor and sliding it up and down the top of my hands just until the blood started to seep through in slits like light through a window blind, I told Dr. Klein.

At home, I read my mother's old copy of *Ordinary People* by Judith Guest. I watched *Irreconcilable Differences* with Drew Barrymore, Shelley Long, and Ryan O'Neal. In English class, I devoured Walt Whitman's *Leaves of Grass*, underlining, photocopying, and dog-earing pages in emotional recognition. I struggled to make sense of things, of my unraveling family unit.

Two

Family History

The gravel crunched under my flats. I was walking across the campus of Oberlin College, part of a group that included my mom, brother, aunt, uncle, cousins, grandfather, and step-grandmother, plus various students and administrators. The wind whipped around me and I pulled my cardigan close, trying not to step on the heels of the people in front of me.

A limestone building in the heart of campus was being named after my grandfather. We'd just finished an introductory ceremony and were headed to the classrooms across the way. I wasn't much younger than the students. I thought about my future college plans as I followed behind my grandfather, a diminutive man with a raspy voice who called my mother, Ellen, "Ellie."

My grandfather, Jesse Philips, was born in 1914 in New York to poor Jewish Hungarian immigrants. He was raised in West Hartford, Connecticut, with his brother, Irving, and sister, Regina. When he was young, he had his sights set on the nearby venerable university, Yale. While he did get in, Yale didn't give him any scholarship money, so he enrolled at the school that gave him the most financial aid: Oberlin in Ohio.

He showed up with twenty-five dollars in his pocket. Cleaning bathrooms and doing dishes, Jesse worked his way through, befriending the janitor so he could study longer in the library, past the typical lights-out hour. He wanted to go to Harvard Law School next but found out they didn't give scholarships to first-year students. He decided on Harvard Business School instead, graduating in 1939, the same year that Germany invaded Poland. When Jesse asked a professor for help getting a job on Wall Street, his teacher shook his head and told him that unless he was from one of the storied German Jewish families like the Lehmans, Kuhns, or Loebs, he didn't stand a chance. Hungarian Jews like him would never get hired. Had he considered retail?

So Jesse settled on a new department store concept that took him to Cincinnati, Ohio. He rose through the ranks, eventually becoming a partner and co-owner until the store was sold to Arthur Beerman.

Meanwhile, he'd aggressively courted my grandmother, ten years younger. A bit heavy and not as pretty as her sister, my grandmother, Carol Jane Frank, despite her quick wit, fabulous writing, and street-smart intellect, didn't have a lot of confidence. Or dates. But she was from a distinguished German Jewish family, the daughter of a stock-broker, Edwin Frank, and Carrie Lorch Frank.

Jesse wasn't a looker. He was shorter than my grandmother and not particularly nice, but he was successful and persistent. Perhaps my grandmother's pedigree appealed to him the most. After she turned him down multiple times, he showed up on her doorstep while she was living at home with her parents and sister and insisted she accompany him on a business trip.

She said, "What the hell," and grabbed a suitcase.

After selling the department store, my grandfather—now a father to my mother, Ellen, and her brother, Tom—purchased a small company that manufactured trailer home windows and doors. Over the next twenty years, he turned it into a publicly traded Fortune 500 manufacturing company called Philips Industries.

At the start of the company's growth, my grandmother decided to help out in the office. She grabbed a bunch of papers from her desk and walked into my grandfather's office, saying, "Jesse—"

My grandfather looked up from his massive desk.

"In the office, you will call me Mr. Philips."

My grandmother looked back at him.

Then she shrugged and said, "I quit."

Jesse ended up becoming a widely revered man, with honors thrust upon him from the US State Department and many universities. He donated a Humanities Center and a gym to Oberlin, where he was a trustee for more than twenty years.

In the dedication ceremony that day, as I looked on, he thanked the janitor for keeping the lights on.

As a husband and a father, he wasn't quite as successful. He wasn't faithful. He wasn't kind. Rumor had it that he impregnated my grandmother's friend.

My grandparents announced their divorce the day after my parents got married in 1971. Soon after, Jesse married Caryl, a woman younger than my mother. The two of them rode horses, competed in yacht races, skied all over the world, and lived a jet-set lifestyle. They doted on their Doberman pinschers, Zeus and Cleo, whose nails I could hear clacking across the massive marble foyer of their modern home in Dayton as they passed by the abstract expressionist paintings. I'd never felt close to my grandfather and, knowing his conflictual relationship with my mom, had always held him at arm's length. But I marveled at the pictures of him with various presidents on the wall as I walked down his stairs to play pool in the basement.

My grandfather had a heart attack while skiing in Alta, Utah, at age eighty, and died from a stroke during the emergency heart surgery. He smoked incessantly until the very end, his raspy voice rattling at every breath as he spoke in his slow, measured way, the smell of nicotine emanating from his suit. Caryl still lives in the house in Dayton.

My grandmother, "Gagy," remarried a rabbi who spent a decade in the air force as a chaplain. Kalman Levitan was a cuddly, warm, clever, and imposing man who would regularly snuggle my grandmother from behind and say, "Do you know how much I love you?"

He carved clocks out of wood, could repair anything broken, played the guitar, collected and printed miniature books (including two of my stories when I was in fourth grade), and was madly in love with my grandmother until the day he died. Her greatest regret, she told me, was that she was in the other room for a minute when he took his final breath. She wasn't holding his hand.

On my father's side, my grandfather, Joseph Schwarzman, was born in Philadelphia to Jewish Austrian immigrants Rebecca and Jacob Schwarzman. Jacob and my grandfather Joe opened Schwarzman's home goods store, which sold towels, cloth napkins, and other dry goods. My grandfather was a tall, gentle soul, with kind, sparkling eyes, who would greet friends by grabbing both of their hands and smiling. He knew every answer on *Jeopardy!* and was a creature of habit, waking up, heading to the store, coming home. He met my grandmother, Arline, when they were both sleepaway camp counselors. Arline, raised by a single mother, Stella, with her sister, Bobbie, in the Bronx, was a fighter, a take-no-prisoners powerhouse who, when she later had my father and his identical twin younger brothers, would throw them all down in the basement so she could clean the house. Once, she told me, she allowed herself to sit on the steps and cry. Not physically or emotionally demonstrative, she exacted perfection, always aspiring for better. She regularly dropped the three boys off at the local library, leaving them to lose themselves in books.

At the end of her life, she had dementia. At the last Thanksgiving we all shared, my uncles and my dad gathered around. One uncle asked my dad how she was doing.

"Not good," my dad replied. "She just told me she loved me."

Everything in their house revolved around the store. My dad and his brothers worked there on weekends when they wanted to be out with their friends, and they supplemented their wallets with odd jobs like lawn mowing. They lived in a neighborhood that soon became overrun by gangs, so they moved out to the suburbs in Abington, Pennsylvania, where my dad became a basketball and track star, one of the fastest boys in all of Pennsylvania.

My dad, unlike my mom's dad, had his sights set on Harvard, not Yale. He only wanted what he believed to be the very best. Yale accepted him and offered him a place on the track team, but Harvard said no. My dad went to a pay phone in his high school and called Harvard's admissions office.

"You've made a huge mistake," he said to the intractable admissions officer. "I'm going to be a huge success and you're going to want me to be a part of your school."

The admissions officer was unmoved.

"If you don't accept me, when I become successful, I'm not going to give you a dime."

My dad saw the opportunity in the home goods market and urged my grandfather, repeatedly, to expand. Why not open up Schwarzman's around the country? He wanted to create an empire like Bed Bath & Beyond would become. My grandfather wasn't interested. My dad couldn't understand. It could be bigger! Better! It just wasn't what my grandfather wanted. He would eventually retire and spend his last decade sailing with my grandmother, racing their tiny sailboat. She moved the rudder and barked orders while he, in his good-natured way, obeyed, content to sail on the seas and look out at the water as those around him aspired to be champions.

My parents met at Harvard Business School. Determined to make money after growing up in a family strapped for cash and being forced to spend all his free time working at "the store," my dad had tried his hand at finance after college and knew he needed more skills. With everyone protesting the Vietnam War and antibusiness sentiment high, he was able to sneak right into HBS despite what he believed were his subpar skills. Finally. Harvard.

My mother, freshly on the East Coast after leaving her home in Dayton, Ohio, and graduating from Northwestern, had gotten a job as a course assistant thanks to her father. He'd shipped her off to Harvard to snag a husband.

My parents were introduced on the steps of Baker Library, my dad going in, my mom coming out, and paused to chat as a mutual friend introduced them. My mom, it turned out, was assigned to grade and edit my dad's papers. They had a whirlwind courtship and got married a year later in Dayton during winter break.

Less than five years later, I was born.

When my dad graduated from Harvard Business School in 1972, newly married to my mom, he headed to Wall Street. The days of the closed German Jewish circles were over and, in the post-Woodstock era when traditional business was frowned upon by most peers his age, my dad had an easy time securing a job with no real experience. He worked at DLJ and Lehman Brothers, quickly becoming a partner and a rising star. The *Wall Street Journal* even wrote a profile about him while he was still in his thirties, which my mother turned into a mirrored version surrounded by round bulbs that could be plugged in and lit up. I thought it was the coolest thing that his picture was in Ken Auletta's book *Greed and Glory on Wall Street*.

I wonder if my father saw in my mother's family a bit of the same prestige and pedigree that had attracted Jesse to Carol. A way up in the world. Perhaps my mother's background made him feel like there was a safety net when he started The Blackstone Group (now simply Blackstone) when I was nine years old. Blackstone has since become a publicly traded company (BX) with more than $700 billion under management.

My family gave me a legacy of entrepreneurship and achievement with multiple role models for innovation, hard work, and creation. At the root of our story is the American Dream and how in multiple generations my family members have come from nothing and risen to the top of their fields, with, perhaps, a leg up from some pretty awesome German Jewish women. We have overcome anti-Semitism and poverty to rise up in the world, to make a difference, when we easily could've succumbed to fate.

If only that janitor who left the library lights on at Oberlin for my grandfather knew how many more people he really helped. I think of him, that unsung hero, as I turn on my library lights to interview authors every single day.

Three

DRINKING: A LOVE STORY

I left Arena. I'm at someone's house."

I was whispering, hiding out in the kitchen of a girl's town house, covertly calling my mother. Just an hour before, my mom had dropped me off at a middle school dance, yelling after me, "Just be yourself, Zib!" Right. Whoever *that* was.

My parents were supposed to pick me up in front of Arena and drive straight out to East Hampton for the weekend. But a girl I barely knew from another school said her parents were out of town. Everyone at the dance seemed to march en masse to her luxurious home around the corner. I didn't want to be left behind, so I followed the crowd.

"You're what? Where are you? Is it a party? Are the parents home?"

I slowly said, "No."

"I get it. You can't talk, right?"

"Right." I nodded.

"Okay, is there alcohol at this party?"

I looked around. In the next room, a blond boy from one of the boys' schools was reaching into a cooler and handing out cans of what I assumed was beer.

"Yes."

"Oh my God."

She sighed.

"Beer? Hard alcohol?"

"The first one."

"Here's what to do. Nurse one beer. Do not drink it, do you hear me? If everyone's drinking and you have to take a drink, just hold the can. Nurse it. Pretend to drink every so often. No one will know the difference."

"Um, okay."

"We'll be there in thirty minutes to pick you up. Okay? Be outside on the street in thirty minutes. And find me the address!"

I squeezed onto the velvet love seat with a few friends and took in the zebra-print walls, an oil painting of a mother and daughter hovering above us, crystal vases on every surface, a deep-pink sheen to the adjoining room.

The blond boy by the cooler turned his attention to me. We locked eyes. He held an unopened beer in his hand and simply pointed at me, eyebrows raised as if to say, "Want one?"

I nodded.

It happened in slow motion. He threw the beer across the room, where it went over, under, over, under, through the light, under the chandelier, and all the way to me, where I extended my hand and caught it.

"Nice!" he said, turning away.

I looked down at the cold beer sweating in my hand and, like my mom had told me, opened it and took a sip. I would nurse it. Just nurse it. Pretend.

Except after a few sips, I started to feel a little something. A little buzz. A little excitement. So I kept drinking. Not pretending. Really doing it. Until I'd guzzled down the contents of the carbonated can. I started giggling. And before I knew it, that cracking whoosh of the beer can opening also forced open the part of me that couldn't talk. I realized that with alcohol, I could be myself. I could laugh. I could be funny.

I could be *me. Where was that in all the books I was reading?* Booze was a best-kept secret. I don't remember the main characters in *Forever* by Judy Blume getting wasted in order to hook up. I'd watch *St. Elmo's Fire* and wonder, "Will I end up like Demi Moore?"

That night, I raced down the elegantly carpeted stairs, past framed photographs of celebrities on the walls, and pulled open the heavy door to the street. My parents were waiting outside in our Volvo, my brother already asleep in the backseat. I got in and slammed the door behind me. As we drove down the side street, I smiled, my nose pressed to the window. I stared up at the town house I'd just left, armed with a magic key I hadn't known existed.

———

By eighth grade, I'd walk into parties all over Manhattan's Upper East Side and head straight to the fridge. There would usually be a six-pack of beer waiting, and I would snag a cool bottle before anyone else could. My ammunition for the evening.

I didn't tell anyone how much I was drinking. I wasn't doing it in private. Everyone else was doing it, too. It was nothing to worry about! I could drink almost a six-pack and not act too loopy. Some kids I knew had started smoking cigarettes or pot. My mother smoked incessantly at home, cigarettes standing sentry in crystal containers strategically placed in every room, so smoking didn't seem remotely appealing to me. Compared with other kids who, at age thirteen, were going downtown to the Limelight club, I was tame. Just beer. Just drinking.

At my new school, kids were drinking for the first time in ninth grade, whereas by then, I was a pro. I was the reigning champion of a drinking game called Quarters. The other girls were all drinking wine coolers and acting giggly afterward at ninth-grade parties. I was showing up with a paper bag I'd gotten from the nearby deli with a six-pack of Coors Light. The guys thought that was cool. I knew it wasn't cool;

it was my talking device, the tool I needed to be who I actually was. Without it, I would be stone silent.

By the time summer vacation arrived in the year of my parents' divorce, I'd gained twenty pounds. I was experiencing depression, something I'd been fighting silently and which would continue to haunt me the rest of my life. After a man on the street catcalled me by saying, "Hey, big girl!" I cracked open.

I sat at my giant white desk in my room swathed in floral fabric and wrote. I wrote about how upset I was that a boy I was interested in didn't like me back, how he'd told a buddy, "But if she lost some weight, she'd be beautiful." I lamented the power the scale held over me, my moods, my life. I hated myself, my lack of willpower, the fact that everyone could see my weakness just by looking at me. My failure was plastered over every pore of my being, an electric sign like in Times Square.

I printed out what I had written to read it myself and my mother intercepted it.

"Zib, this is amazing," she said, walking into my bedroom immersed in the pages.

My mom was always dressed nicely. So nicely, in fact, that my classmate in third grade told me I had the best-dressed mom around. When I told my mom, she was so flattered that she put her hand over her chest and said dramatically, "Meeee?"

A Chanel dress. A sweater around her shoulders with khakis and sneakers. A suit. Always put together.

"Mom! That was private!"

"No, no, you have to publish this, Zib! Other girls need to see it. It's really good."

My mom persuaded me to try to sell it. We looked up the address of *Seventeen* magazine and sent it in cold. They bought it. Two years later the essay ran with a giant picture of me holding a scale in disgust. It came out while I was away at Bennington College for the summer taking photography and fiction writing courses. I was reading *A Prayer for Owen Meany* and had listened to John Irving as he spoke to our whole program the night before. *Seventeen*, *Sassy*, and *YM* magazines were my go-tos. I would soak up their personal essays desperately, like a fish gulping for air.

Sitting on the giant lawn, surrounded by a few close friends from the program, I opened the FedEx envelope and pulled out the glossy magazine. I flipped and flipped until . . .

Oh!

There I was!

It felt surreal. Me looking at me, my words spilling off the page.

"That's so cool, Zibs!" my friend Karen, a redhead from Philly, said. "Mazel tov!"

I just shook my head.

"How crazy, right?" I responded.

I wasn't nervous. I didn't feel exposed or brave. I knew that sharing my feelings was the right thing to do. I just knew there were other girls who felt the same way I did, who were stuck inside their souls, carrying around the loneliness of their feelings without realizing their universality. I've been writing for those girls ever since.

———

My selective mutism and social anxiety got worse after my parents' divorce. The summer after I wrote that essay about my weight, I went on a monthlong French immersion program. I lived with a French family in Saint-Rémy-de-Provence in the South of France in July while taking three hours of French classes every morning and living like a true Francophile the rest of the time. Before and after, I traveled with the twenty kids from New York to cities and landmarks in France like the Loire Valley, Versailles, and Paris.

I wanted to be in French honors class, so I worked all summer, wrote letters to my teacher back in New York, and studied so hard that by the end of the summer, I was dreaming in French.

I could speak in class and around my "family," which owned a beautiful villa with a pool and served fresh bread and yogurt for dessert after the salad course and took me to the beach on weekends. But when I was with the group? Forget it. The girls on the program were all one or two years older than me. Two of them befriended each other right away and were inseparable from day one. Two guys I knew from school started dating girls on the trip and barely had time to say hello. I didn't pair up with anyone. I was left out. And sober. If any of us were caught drinking on the program, we would be sent home immediately. I'm sure other kids found a way, but the idea of being expelled from my summer program for drinking was enough to stop me in my tracks.

When I wasn't speaking in class, I was silent. On all the group adventures, I would sit alone on the bus, the other kids laughing, kissing, and hooting and hollering around me. But I'd just sit there, secretly coveting their social skills.

I couldn't talk. I didn't want to eat. I felt isolated, alone. My parents' divorce was finalized while I was away; they told me on one of my phone calls home. I lost all the weight I'd gained that school year.

By the final week of the trip, I was so depressed I couldn't stay awake. I wanted to remain in bed and sleep all the time, which wasn't an option. I started sleeping on my feet. I walked through most of Versailles with my eyes closed, the group leader guiding me through. I read on the bus trips and late at night: *L'étranger* by Albert Camus, *Huis clos* by Jean-Paul Sartre. I wrote in English and in French.

I dreamed of coming home.

I dreamed of being able to be comfortable.

I turned to writing for help.

By my junior year of high school, everyone seemed to have paired up with older boys. Not me. I had a few short relationships and hook-ups, but nothing serious. My girlfriends were suddenly less accessible. I grew increasingly depressed, especially as the strife inside my home demanded all my attention. Things were not going smoothly on the divorce front.

On Valentine's Day in my high school, roses were for sale and all the gorgeous girls ran around showing off their flowers from admiring boys. I didn't get any roses. I sat in the armchair in the student lobby lounge with my crew of friends, all in relationships, and wrote in my black-and-white journal. I read *Like Water for Chocolate* by Laura Esquivel and fell asleep at night feeling sorry for myself.

I also took photographs constantly. I became the photo editor of my yearbook and snapped shots at sports events, plays, and during classes. On Saturdays, I'd go into the darkroom at school, soaking papers in liquids until images appeared like ghosts. Observing came naturally to me. The camera gave me another tool. Something to do. To say. Something to give me a purpose. Years later, I would pore over every page of *Shutterbabe: Adventures in Love and War* by author and photographer Deborah Copaken Kogan.

I also threw myself into team sports and ended up being co-captain of all my teams in both tennis and lacrosse. (I'd read *Chris Evert, the Young Champion*, by Lynn Haney, over and over again growing up, wanting to be her.)

When the time for college applications came along, I decided I wanted to go to Brown. I didn't want to try for Yale. I felt that if I got in, it would have been only because of my dad. I wanted to prove my own merit. Well, the college counselor didn't think Brown was going to be a fit, what with my legacy status at Yale. She pushed that option hard. I got into Yale, but was wait-listed at Brown. I didn't feel like I deserved to get in. Kids in my class who were much smarter than me had been rejected. It didn't seem fair. I wasn't the A student or Latin expert or debate champion. I had a solid A-/B+ average. That didn't feel stellar enough to get into the best schools around. And yet, I decided to accept.

I vowed to prove that I was smart enough to go there, that I could work harder than anyone, and that I could contribute to Yale. (Later, I would spend countless hours upstairs in the Davenport library, hand-writing review sheets as my girlfriends chatted with boys at the more social, subterranean Cross Campus Library. I ended up graduating cum laude, with honors, and being the editor in chief of *The Insider's Guide to the Colleges*, an entirely student-written college guidebook published by St. Martin's Press. That doesn't mean I should've been admitted over those other students, but at least I proved I could keep up.)

O

1994–2001

Four

THE DEVIL WEARS PRADA

Ijust met the most adorable girl and I know you two are going to be friends."

My mom clasped her hands together in excitement. It was move-in day and we were starting the process of lugging boxes out of the station wagon up to my dorm room.

"Oh please. Come on, Mom," I said. "Let me make my own friends. Are you just in there talking to strangers?"

But my mother was right. I walked through the giant archway and onto the massive freshman quad called Old Campus. There was Stacey in a white T-shirt, gray shorts, and Nikes, her hair puffy and curly.

"Hi! I'm Stacey," she said, her eyes shining.

"I hear you met my mom," I said.

She laughed.

"Yep. Mine already left. Need help with your bags?"

I'd had visions of creating a whole new identity for myself, falling madly in love like in *Love Story* by Erich Segal. Who knew the real love of my life would appear like this on day one?

Stacey helped my dad; my mom; my younger brother, Teddy; and me pull the containers, suitcases, and boxes across campus and upstairs. She was outgoing, with a huge smile, confidence, and a magnetic sense of who she was. She was taller than me, with an athletic build from rowing and, as she would say, "pretty awesome legs." Stace had a mass of curly brown hair that had a life of its own. Later she'd end up spending hours getting it professionally straightened, blow-drying it, tending to it as if it were a small pet. She loved her perky boobs and later, when we were living together, often walked around half naked with no self-consciousness. Her pale skin, searing blue eyes, straight nose, and wide smile gave her a 1950s glamour girl elegance—not a traditional beauty, and yet a knockout. She truly commanded a room when she entered it; everyone was drawn to her bright light, energy, and effusive personality, the mischievous twinkle in her eye that dared us to follow her.

I was hooked.

Back then, I felt the exact opposite way about myself. I hated my body, hated that I always had to be so careful about what I ate, hated that my physique, while athletic and strong, seemed shaped for child-bearing as soon as I turned ten years old. I could've been cast as an extra in *Fiddler on the Roof*, but I did not look like the other students partying at Naples Pizza, the local beer-and-pizza place at Yale. My curvy body, although never significantly overweight, had also made me feel different from the long, lean girls I grew up with at my all-girls' private school on the East River of Manhattan.

Developing early had mortified me. My mother had taken me to the lingerie floor of Bergdorf Goodman, a swanky department store on Fifth Avenue, for my first bra. At age ten, I'd hidden between the silk nightgowns and robes on a nearby clothing rack as she asked for help. I was always covering up, modest. Years later, when I tried out to be a walk-on to the Yale women's lacrosse team, I took one look at the communal shower setup and quit.

Stacey was off to crew practice the first day I met her. She'd been recruited from Andover, a top New England boarding school, so was used to dorm life. She ate with her team after practice. Meanwhile,

I was so homesick that after a few weeks, I started sneaking back to Manhattan.

I called home late one afternoon, sitting alone at my desk in a tiny dorm room on the fifth floor of a lonely stone tower, the damp New Haven air chilling me to the bone. I was reading Marcel Proust's *In Search of Lost Time* in my literature class and dreaming of madeleines, which made me miss my mother's chocolate chip brownies. Stacey was busy. I was too embarrassed to walk across the entire campus up to Davenport, my residential college, and the dining room I was assigned to eat in. Who would I sit with? (All Yale freshmen lived together on a quad called Old Campus, but we would split off for dinner to go to one of the twelve residential colleges to which we were assigned, and where we would live during sophomore year.)

Although I'd managed to do it a few times, I hated it. The thought of crossing campus, walking past groups of other students all by myself in the cold, entering that imposing Gothic dining hall with six-foot-tall oil portraits on the mahogany walls, and seeing dozens of seemingly relaxed and happy students all lined up and in conversation at long oak tables in heavy, hard-to-move chairs made me panic.

By October, I couldn't stand it anymore.

I called home.

"Hi, Mom," I said, rearranging my assignments on my desk, trying to sound normal. "What are you guys having for dinner?"

"Hi, Zib! Swordfish and roast potatoes. Why do you ask?"

I could picture her standing in the kitchen of our apartment on the Upper East Side, twirling the phone cord around her finger. She'd recently quit smoking after twenty years and was always fidgeting with something. She was probably writing the next day's grocery list with a pencil on the monogrammed blue notepads dotting the house. It would smell like roasting garlic and herbs in the kitchen, and closer to the front door, across the marble foyer with the trompe l'oeil paintings of open windows overlooking fictitious fields and flowers, would be a heavily scented candle. Potpourri in bowls. It drove me crazy that my family lived so formally. I wanted an informal, cozy environment like my friend Rebecca's family apartment on the Upper West Side, not a swanky, heavily decorated apartment with window shades so thick I had to pull them closed with both hands.

And yet as soon as I was gone, I longed to be back.

"I'm on my way."

That night I enjoyed a dinner served on a giant silver tray from which my mother carefully doled out servings of *haricots verts* with matching silver spoons, my brother and I flanking her at the head of a dining room table big enough for twenty people. After dinner I said goodbye and drove in the dark toward my dorm. The only thing pulling me back there was the prospect of sitting on the multicolored rag rug Stacey had brought from boarding school. It had become our evening ritual, after which I would trudge across the hall, climb under my light-blue-and-white duvet, and read books like Susanna Kaysen's *Girl, Interrupted* and *The Virgin Suicides* by Jeffrey Eugenides.

———

Stace and I were assigned rooms across the hall from each other that first year and then lived together the next three years, first in an on-campus dorm room so small that one of us had to sit on the bottom bunk for the other to squeeze out between the dresser and the bed, and then for two years in an off-campus apartment with our friend Abby. We even spent the summers living together in New York. Stacey, with her infectious energy, sparkling eyes, and party-girl attitude, quickly became a part of my family. She came home with me for vacations and trips, and even lived in my brother's room for a while.

Sometimes I wondered what she saw in me. I mean, she was this popular, bubbly, strong girl who always had friends popping over to visit, scrawling notes on the whiteboard on our front door if she wasn't home. While I had friends, I was much more reserved. I studied a lot. I didn't like to drink during the day, so I skipped tailgating. I was too shy to interact with upperclassmen, needed a few vodka-cranberries to even talk to guys at parties (and many more to do anything else), and preferred reading to goofing around.

And yet somehow we complemented each other. When Stace failed her economics test and was too upset to tell her dad, I hugged and consoled her and helped her make review sheets and a timetable for studying. When she tried to go out without a coat in the freezing cold because it would mess up her outfit, I'd make her wear one, and she'd kiss me on the cheek and dash out. She drew me out of my shell, pulling me along, opening me up. We were like an old married couple, and we spent hours talking, laughing, studying, chatting, and writing notes to slip under each other's doors. Sending each other postcards if we were separated. Emailing constantly during our summer jobs. She was my person.

One summer weekend at my mom's house in East Hampton, where I'd been spending weekends and summers since 1979, Stacey and two other friends, Abby and Rebecca, spent the weekend. We stayed up late, dancing in the kitchen and trying on my mom's reading glasses and cracking up. We stood on the blue hand-painted chairs with their braided wood seats. Stacey was doing her signature dance, pointing her index fingers up while looking at the ceiling.

"Girls, time to go skinny-dipping!" Stacey announced, putting her hand on the door to the backyard.

"No way," I said, shaking my head. "Not a chance."

"Come on, Zibs! You'll never forget it!"

"Zibs, let's do it!" Abby added.

"I'll go first!" Stacey said.

Of course she would.

I lagged behind the three girls as they stripped and dove into the pool. I walked outside holding a pile of plush blue towels for everyone and watched as they bobbed in the blackness.

"Come on, get in!" Stacey yelled.

Should I?

"Okay, fine," I said, "but you all have to close your eyes until I'm in."

"Okay, okay," they said.

"Just get in!"

I peeled off my shimmery "going out" tank top and black pants and raced down the shallow-end steps to the water, shocking in its full-body grip.

"Yay, Zibs!" Stacey called out.

I swam over to them, treading water in the deep end under the moonlight, as the four of us glistened in the darkness, our laughter bouncing off the pool walls. It was just one time of many when Stacey's influence would weave its way into the waters of my psyche.

———

I couldn't figure out what I wanted to do during my college summers. I wanted to be a writer. I'd known that since I was nine years old. I just didn't know how to do it. No one was recruiting for personal essayists. I'd read Phillip Lopate's anthology *The Art of the Personal Essay*, and Anne Lamott's *Bird by Bird*, looking for instruction.

I decided to try a few ways in.

After my freshman year at Yale, Marie Brenner, a *Vanity Fair* editor at large and family friend, recommended me for an internship at *Vanity Fair*. I was beyond excited about working at such a glossy magazine, one that had great, substantive articles and that I loved to read.

I spent that summer of 1995 at Condé Nast, rotating between departments. I started in Events with a gray-haired British lady, Sara Marks, who was often meeting with PR guru Beth Kseniak. Two younger journalists would pop in and out of our tiny office space: Aimée Bell and Matt Tyrnauer. (Aimée is now the head of Gallery Books.)

"Can you get Bob Colacello on the phone?" Sara would ask.

"Sure," I'd say, thumbing through the Rolodex on the counter. Bob who? How did I even spell that?

I moved from Events into Features with Jane Sarkin. I sat on her carpeted floor at the low glass coffee table and clipped pictures of stars she wanted in the Hollywood issue. Jane was often on the phone, including once to ask her doctor if she could schedule her upcoming C-section around the timing of the next big issue.

Fashion came next. While I was tasked with slipping tiny square slides into their plastic sleeves and inserting them into notebooks, the fashion team raced around the office, led by Elizabeth Saltzman, a tall, athletic, regal-looking brunette whose stiletto heels meant business. A tall, blonde assistant who sat outside Elizabeth's office had a Chihuahua that would scamper under my rolling desk chair.

The assistant gave me an endless list of errands, including taking a black town car with piles of garment bags on my lap and dropping them off at a Midtown fashion designer's office. I'd taken town cars in my private life: my parents insisted I take a Skyline credit ride car whenever I went downtown. The subway was strictly prohibited.

But the town car trips I took during that summer felt like chariot rides down the gold-paved roads of Oz. I felt so important taking a car for work.

At the end of my internship, Elizabeth flung open her office door like Vanna White to reveal piles of costume jewelry covering the carpet.

"Take whatever you want!" she said.

I still have a fake giant pearl bracelet I snagged that day. It's one of my most fabulous possessions. When Lauren Weisberger's *The Devil Wears Prada* came out, chronicling her time in the clutches of Condé Nast, I was like, "Yes! This!" A fellow magazine-world warrior.

In my rotation with business manager Susan Goodall, I worked with author contracts. I'd pull out the giant drawers and run my fingers over the files, each containing an author's name. Leslie Bennetts. Bryan Burrough. Amy Fine Collins. Michael Shnayerson. How could I become one of them instead of the girl dropping off dresses for the fashion department? Once or twice, I got to meet editor in chief Graydon Carter as he charged through the office.

Did I want a life in which I had to schedule my C-section around a particular magazine issue? I loved the collaborative feel, the buzz, the energy, the celebrity infusion, the sense that we were making a difference in the world. But I realized I didn't want to be a magazine editor after all. I wanted to be the writer whose contract was stuffed in a file cabinet.

The following summer, obsessed with the classes I was taking as part of my psychology major, I decided to work in the adolescent inpatient unit at a psychiatric hospital. Maybe I wanted to be a psychologist! I'd watched Dudley Moore's *Crazy People*, which was a hilarious take on both advertising and psychology. *Awakenings* by Oliver Sacks and *The Bell Jar* by Sylvia Plath both captivated me with their tales of psychiatric descent and resurrection. I thought I could make a difference. I helped with the psychiatric care of inpatients not much younger than me. Many patients were just bouncing back and forth between "juvie" and the inpatient unit, trying hard to earn "points," which converted to privileges. A few were mentally impaired, including one boy who could only grunt, and another who was covered in hair and would lunge at us with such frequency that he'd have to be restrained, an alarm sounding throughout the unit.

A skinny, soulful Black girl was there for depression. *That* I could relate to. I sat with her on the couch in the common room as she cried, listening, echoing her feelings, helping her get through it. Later, she told me how much it had helped. Nothing else I did there seemed to make a difference. The system itself seemed unfair, resistant to change.

A few weeks after my internship ended, I sat at the breakfast table at my mom's apartment and picked up the *New York Post*. The mug shots of two former patients stared back at me. They'd just gotten arrested for stealing a car.

The following summer I tried something new again. Maybe I'd like advertising? I did love brands and had been mailing letters to places like Colgate and Clairol since I was young, the same way I'd written fan mail to authors. My final summer in college I lived with Stacey in my stepfather Howard's old apartment (he had recently moved in with and gotten engaged to my mom) and interned at Ogilvy & Mather advertising on the Fisher-Price, Kodak, and Maxwell House accounts.

On the first day in my office—which was actually the A/V closet—my boss, Pat, popped her head in the door and asked me to research the "365 degrees of Coke."

"Look it up on the World Wide Web," she said, whizzing back into the hallway.

The what?

I loved that summer in brand planning. I loved analyzing consumer behavior, understanding brands, applying trends, finding the most important parts of products to include in the creative briefs. I read *Understanding Brands*, edited by Don Cowley, and Paco Underhill's *Why We Buy: The Science of Shopping*. I decided that the fast pace fit me better than the long days inside a psychiatric hospital or even the magazine world. There was something fundamental I instinctively understood about branding. Logos. Design. The visual element. The emotional aspect of sales. I was all in.

Five

What It Takes

It was a meet-cute for the movies. During Christmas break of sophomore year at Yale, I watched my younger brother, Teddy, play an indoor lacrosse match at Chelsea Piers. The cavernous indoor arena nestled along the Hudson River had multiple fields of fake grass all lined up next to each other. High school boys clanked their sticks together as they sprinted back and forth, but there were hardly any fans. My brother was playing on one field. On the shared sidelines, I started chatting with another older sibling home from college, Josh, who was watching his brother on the next field. We chatted the whole time, swapping names of friends we both knew, talking about college and our families.

At the end, he said, "Hey, if you're in town this week, we should meet up for dinner."

"That would be fun," I said, smiling.

I hesitated.

"I do have a boyfriend, though," I added. I'd started dating a classmate who was on the swim team.

"No problem," he said.

We met up in the city later that week and he whisked me downtown to Little Italy for a romantic night of pasta and cannoli. Josh seemed to be my dream guy—a nice Jewish boy who had grown up just a few blocks away from me. This was it. We were two peas in a pod. And yet, I was dating someone else. I said goodbye at the end of the night and made sure to save his number.

For over a year, Josh would call and check in periodically.

"Hey, still got that boyfriend?"

"Yep," I'd answer.

"Okay. Bye!"

Until one time he called and I could finally say, "Not anymore."

We were together for the next three years. Josh was a year older than me and was moving to Los Angeles for the entertainment strategy job he'd already accepted when we started dating. I accompanied him on his many trips out west to get set up and even helped him find his first apartment above the Sunset Strip in West Hollywood; we made plans for me to move in after graduation. In the interim, I suggested his old friend from college move in, which he did, to hold my place.

I'd thought seriously about becoming a clinical psychologist and getting a PhD. I had immersed myself in the research side of my psychology degree, even running a study on the application of social comparison theory to eating disorders and working at the Yale Center for Eating and Weight Disorders and the Yale Conduct Clinic. But it wasn't going to work. Josh wanted me to come out to LA for two years and then follow him back east to go to business school. After that, we'd end up somewhere for good. Could I wait to start a PhD program then? I doubted I would want to after all that time had gone by, but I put a pin in the process and decided to work in advertising again. The only advertising-adjacent job I could find after graduation, however, was at a tiny brand development and design firm in a former motor inn in Studio City.

One of only ten employees, I had my own office and many responsibilities. I could go to all the business meetings with my boss, Nancy, and the company cofounder, but I would also be working on the design side of the business, communicating with clients and sharing their zillions of changes with the design team. Soon I learned how to push back a bit and explain why the designers did certain things. I knew if I walked into the design studio too many times on behalf of a given client, I'd be met with eye rolls and indignation.

For one client pitch, I had to put together a competitive roundup of internet companies. I realized that many of them were based nearby in Pasadena. Maybe I'd have more fun being on the client side? I could be part of the start-up instead of the one asking the start-ups to hire us for their branding campaigns.

I applied online to idealab!, an internet incubator, through the form on its site. Miraculously, I got the job of assistant marketing manager.

I was the twenty-fifth employee at the open-plan, loftlike company, where desks were actually wooden doors supported by file cabinets. Knowledge sharing between all the start-ups that the incubator was launching was one of my main responsibilities. These were companies like eToys, PetSmart, Citysearch, Cooking.com, GoTo, CarsDirect, MusicNow, and PayMyBills.

I organized breakfasts for the marketing and business development teams and the CEOs. I made the name tags, booked the restaurants, planned the events, and took notes. While the CEOs strategized about their businesses, I'd sit quietly away from the main table, my back flat against the wall. Leaning in wasn't yet a thing. From my wallflower vantage, I soaked up all the knowledge I could. On the side, I bolstered my business acumen with books like Howard Schultz's *Pour Your Heart into It: How Starbucks Built a Company One Cup at a Time.*

As the company grew from 25 employees in one office to 250 employees in five worldwide locations, I was a marketing resource to everyone who joined. For fun, I volunteered to plan the company holiday party at the Ritz-Carlton and threw a pseudo-wedding with lavish gift bags and a band, dinner, and dancing. I organized keg parties at the office on Friday afternoons.

Soon my entire social and professional life revolved around idealab!. We all had stock options and thought we'd be worth millions of dollars.

Whenever any of our operating companies would go public, we would watch the stock price rise all day.

As the outward face of the company's marketing team, I took most of the meetings with companies that wanted to partner with idealab!: vendors from affiliate marketing companies and magazines like the *Industry Standard*, which wanted a piece of idealab!'s business. I organized a two-million-dollar online advertising campaign for the operating companies, gifted for the holidays by founder Bill Gross. While in London to celebrate the millennium with my dad, Stacey, Abby, and Rebecca, I sat in our hotel room and sent daily detailed tracking reports to all the marketing managers.

The company, like many of the casualties of the internet boom and bust, never went public.

———

Two of my pet peeves have always been when people speak too slowly or when meetings go on needlessly for too long. At idealab!, my boss had to take me aside once after a group meeting.

We ducked into one of the glass conference rooms, all named after islands I'd never heard of, like Santorini.

"Do you realize how many times you rolled your eyes? Especially when Joan was speaking?"

"Oh no! I did?"

I covered my face with embarrassment. I didn't think I'd shown anyone how irritated I'd been. I just didn't see the point in all these useless meetings. I'd always hated group projects, preferring to get everything done on my own or, at least, divide responsibilities clearly and have ownership over an entire piece.

"Yes. Zibby, I know Joan can be a little inefficient and all over the place, but she's good friends with our founder," my boss said. "You have to be a little more patient with her while she learns the ropes. Not everyone is supersmart like you."

I apologized and disabused her of the notion that I was some kind of genius. I was walking away when she followed up with, "And watch the eye-rolling!"

———

Josh and I hadn't banked on his roommate not wanting to move out when I arrived. Eventually, we moved to Laurel Canyon, to a small house on Wonderland Avenue. I would read about Wonderland in many novels and memoirs, including, years later, Stephanie Danler's *Stray: A Memoir*. We stayed only a few months before finding out that, years prior, people had been murdered two houses away. I broke the lease and found us another place in West Hollywood, where JLo also had an apartment.

———

I would've done anything for Josh. Now *this* was love. I adored his family. We got each other. But he was working around the clock in Los Angeles and I was in Pasadena attending and planning keg parties. With Josh, I was clearly second fiddle. He was working insane hours in a rigorous, prestigious job. Everything was about his career. That was clear and, at his age, understandable. He was worth it, I told myself. I was in love!

As months went by, Josh and I barely saw each other. We were drifting apart, ships passing in the night. Plus once I had a taste of my own career, I couldn't get enough. And the more into my work I got, the less I wanted to be someone's supporting actor. The timing, it seemed, just wasn't right.

Then I started to fall for one of the CEOs of one of our operating companies. Matthew. Someone who saw me in action at work and thought I was awesome. We started emailing, hanging out in groups, getting to know each other. His attention was intermittent, but when he turned on his bright light, it was intoxicating. I hate to admit that

I like to have the next mate lined up before I say goodbye to the old, but I seem to follow that pattern. I am not proud of it, but there it is.

Josh and I broke up. Even though I knew it was the right decision at the time, I was hysterical. I'd been so sure we were going to get married. I'd loved him so much. Sometimes I wonder if that love ever really goes away or if it just morphs into something else in the universe. I mean, where does it go? I feel that love swirling around as I greet his mother on the street or hug his brothers hello at events in New York. It never just disappears.

Josh moved out of our apartment and onto his friend's couch while I looked for a new apartment. I was distracted. Disjointed. I got into car accidents. I lost my purse, twice. I almost got hit by a car. No one back home could believe we'd broken up. I read *Heartburn* by Nora Ephron and tried to escape my own life by climbing Everest in *Into Thin Air* by Jon Krakauer.

Stacey came out to visit as soon as I told her what had happened. She helped me pack up the plates and bowls Josh and I had lovingly bought together at Crate & Barrel. What was I doing with my life? I was only twenty-three years old, but I felt ancient. Stace helped me get set up in a new apartment down the street, reassuring me it would all work out.

Eventually, I couldn't take it anymore. I asked our COO if I could transfer to the newly formed New York office. She agreed. I needed my family and friends. I was tired of spending nights alone in my apartment, hoping a friend would call me to go out. I wanted to go home.

I'd tried once before to get a promotion, but the COO had turned me down. I was doing more than almost anyone at that point, throwing myself into my job with all my heart and soul, yet I was getting paid less than all the marketing managers at the operating companies.

Sitting across the desk, I explained to her why I should be earning more money. I gave a thoughtful, analytical presentation that included competitive salary information.

She looked at me across the desk, steely-eyed, and then gave a lopsided smile.

"But, Zibby," she said. "You have such a nice car."

Silence.

I remembered driving past her the other morning, parking my silver Saab convertible in the company garage.

"My car was a gift," I replied carefully. "It has nothing to do with how much I deserve to be paid for my work."

She snorted.

I didn't get the raise.

I don't think she was sad to see me go.

Soon I was settling into my new position in New York, having recently moved back in with Stacey and Sarah, one of my oldest girlfriends, who actually gave me the nickname Zibby when we were in a baby playgroup together. One day, I was walking through the lower Broadway office when my boss leaned back in his Aeron chair and gestured for me to come over.

He pointed to his computer screen.

"Do you know this guy?"

My dad had just bought a new apartment in a prestigious New York City co-op for a price that made news.

"Here we go again," I thought. How was I supposed to respond?

"That's my dad," I said quietly.

My new boss bolted upright, both feet on the floor.

"Wow, I was kidding. I was just asking because of your last name."

"It's okay. Don't worry about it," I said.

My boss never looked at me the same way again, nor did anyone in the office after they all casually popped by his computer that day, looking from the screen over to me and back again.

I'd gotten used to that kind of thing. But it still hurt.

Since 1985, I'd had a front-row seat as my dad turned Blackstone into a leading player in the financial world. As Blackstone's stock value rose from a low of $3.88 to over $150.00, my dad's value also rose. He went from raking leaves, working in the store for extra cash, and living in roach-infested New York City walk-ups without enough cash to treat his dates to a proper dinner, to never having to worry about money.

At almost seventy-five years old, my dad still works nonstop, although he'll always duck out of a meeting if I call to say hello. He gets his energy from innovating and creating, building businesses, seeing new opportunities, evaluating things logically, and then, when he feels it's risk-free, entering new markets.

He has also been just as innovative in his philanthropy, giving away a huge percentage of what he has earned. He has donated buildings like the Stephen A. Schwarzman Building at the New York Public Library and the new Schwarzman Center at Yale University. He started programs like the Schwarzman Scholars in China and an artificial intelligence institute at M.I.T., and has made countless other donations to people in need that will never make the news.

I am well aware of my privilege, especially the fact that I was randomly lucky to be born into this family. The fact that I'm white has given me even more unfair advantages in today's world. I strive to do the best I can for the world with everything I have, to use my fortune for good, support organizations that I admire like my family does, and not squander anything.

As my family's wealth has exploded, the Blackstone stock continually rising, I've been incredulous. For a long time I tried to keep that part of my life a secret, asking my dad's driver to drop me off two blocks away from school so my classmates wouldn't see, or occasionally fudging how I got to the Hamptons for the weekend when really I'd flown on a helicopter.

The cat appears to be out of the bag now, despite my different last name. I'm insanely proud of my dad and his accomplishments. If I've learned nothing else from reading and talking with authors, it's the corrosive power of secret keeping, something that propels many works of fiction and memoir. I don't want to hide it anymore, but I would never flaunt it. That's just not who I am.

I don't spend money on superficial things like expensive clothes or on my appearance, except for highlights to hide the gray (nonnegotiable). I don't see a swanky dermatologist or get Botox. I carry tote bags I've received for free or with my company's logo, not a Birkin. I've chosen to allocate my resources to giving back, supporting others, donating to meaningful charities, building businesses, and creating beautiful, warm, open, inviting homes filled with colorful photographs, cozy fabrics, and livable spaces. Then I fling open the front door so everyone else can enjoy them, too, greeting my guests with a hug and warm smile. It's my duty to share what I have in every way. I want everyone to enjoy it. My dad shared his own story in *What It Takes: Lessons in the Pursuit of Excellence* in 2019. His solid values and ethos are literally written in the book, a series of life lessons at the end. Interviewing my dad was my favorite podcast of all.

Six

QUARTERLIFE CRISIS

I worked in Trump Tower before it became infamous. That first year back in New York, I left my job at idealab! and took a consumer products marketing position at Unilever Prestige, where I worked on the launch of the Vera Wang fragrance. I took *the* escalator up to my office every day.

Back at the apartment on the Upper West Side that I shared with Stacey and Sarah, Stacey was looking for a new job after getting laid off—along with many coworkers—from Organic. She would sometimes proudly exhibit a chicken she'd roasted for us when we got home from work. Other times Stace would be in one of her super-trendy outfits, like a pale-pink Michael Stars top and a black pencil skirt with three-inch strappy high heels, racing out the door to meet one of her legions of fans or other close friends. Or the three of us would order in Chinese food and sit for hours at the dining room table, coming up with business ideas and commiserating about our love lives. *Confessions of a Shopaholic* by Sophie Kinsella hadn't come out yet, but it was that sensibility—girls in our twenties trying hilariously to hack our way through life—that colored our conversations. We watched—and read— *Sex and the City* by Candace Bushnell as if it were our job.

It was at our dining room table that I had an idea. I wanted to create a service to help the incoming throngs of Wall Street analysts and associates get their new apartments set up and "decorated," and their phone and cable installed, since they were too busy to deal with it. I'd just done that for a college friend of mine, Jeremy, and thought I could scale the service. A nice perk, I thought, could be actually meeting a guy that way. Tons of ancillary benefits! I only really knew about what was going on in those office towers from accounts like *Liar's Poker* by Michael Lewis, a book I adored.

I decided to ask my dad for his advice.

Over lunch at his table at the now-defunct Four Seasons restaurant, the power spot in Midtown for which I always got dressed up, he listened to my pitch.

"Well, Zib," he said. "It's not a *bad* idea. But before you start a business, you should probably know what you're doing."

I was ready to go back to school for something, but I didn't want to commit to a five-year PhD program. For the previous few years, I'd missed being overwhelmed and busy, being in a community of supersmart people, even being stressed. I was good at that. I was *used* to that. Compared with the intensity of my academic life, I didn't find my post-college work challenging enough. After years of killing myself around the clock to achieve at school, I'd walk out of the office in the early evenings with nothing left on my to-do list and think, "Now what?" I'd plow through giant books like *I Know This Much Is True* by Wally Lamb because I could.

Perhaps, my dad suggested, I should go to business school.

How could I resist this coming-full-circle moment? If it weren't for Harvard Business School, I wouldn't exist. Even though my parents got divorced when I was fourteen, my origin story seemed prophetic. So I shelved my business idea and studied for the GMATs—the required standardized test to get into business school—with Stacey, who also decided to apply.

Stace and I took our GMATs at the same time and place, separated by just one booth. (She scored ten points higher than I did.) But right before we submitted our applications, Stacey, thanks to a former colleague, got a new consulting job at Marsh, a division of Marsh and McLennan. She was very excited about it—and figured she could use a little more job experience on her résumé—so decided to wait a year to apply. Reluctantly, I applied to business schools without her, but I made her promise that she'd try to meet me at whichever school I picked.

I hated leaving Stacey behind in New York. I didn't want to go anywhere without her. I left behind my copy of *Quarterlife Crisis: The Unique Challenges of Life in Your Twenties* by Alexandra Robbins and Abby Wilner. Our bible.

———

On the spring night when I found out I'd been accepted to HBS, I went out in the West Village with a group of girlfriends. It was an eyeliner kind of night. I'd been mostly single for the past year. I couldn't seem to meet anyone in New York and things with that CEO hadn't lasted.

I'd get dressed up each weekend night, often with Stacey and Sarah, and find myself in crowded bars and clubs, smooshed against strangers. I'd eye random guys, sometimes catch their attention, and think, "Who *are* these guys?"

I wasn't ever going to meet someone this way. We didn't even know we needed *All the Rules: Time-Tested Secrets for Capturing the Heart of Mr. Right* by Ellen Fein and Sherrie Schneider.

And yet, when Saturday nights rolled around, I couldn't help myself. *What if my future husband is waiting at the bar that my girlfriends are going to and I miss meeting him? What about all those kids who would never be born!*

So I'd drag myself off the couch, put down *Memoirs of a Geisha* by Arthur Golden, or Frank McCourt's *Angela's Ashes*, or perhaps Rebecca

Wells's *Divine Secrets of the Ya-Ya Sisterhood*, and try to wear something revealing enough to show I was on the market, yet conservative enough to show I wasn't that kind of girl.

Stacey would often wrap a bright-red boa around her neck as we went out. She clacked about in her super-high heels as she got ready to go out, blasting Dido or eighties music in the house while she did her eye makeup, always perfectly framing her bright-blue eyes. She always knew what to wear, while I would spend forever in my closet, trying things on, then throwing them onto a growing pile on the floor. Nothing ever looked good.

Stace was dating a basketball player for a few months during a hiatus from her long-term relationship with Bryan, who she had been dating during college and whom we all adored. We all had a feeling they'd get back together but needed some time apart before committing to each other. The basketball player never came over and rarely went out with us. I didn't like it. I felt like the concerned sitcom father with his arms crossed over his chest, saying, "If he cares, why won't he come meet me? Eh?"

Yet Stacey would always rush over to his place when he called. She had stocked our kitchen shelves with canned peaches and would grab a can on her way out the door, winking at me.

"You never know," she'd say, and give me a quick kiss on the cheek.

I was too embarrassed to ask her what *exactly* she and the basketball guy did with them.

On the nights we went out together, she had no qualms about talking to other guys. I needed a few drinks before even contemplating it.

When I got into business school, I let out a sigh of dating relief. I'd meet someone at school! I didn't have to worry anymore. I could just go out and have fun with my friends without obsessing that my potential lifelong mate was perhaps in the bathroom line at every restaurant we went to. I stopped thinking about it.

Of course, that's when I met Charlie.

It was our third stop of the night. We'd been bopping around the West Village, including one house party, and decided to make our last stop a popular hangout called Tortilla Flats. A Mexican restaurant with a few diner-style tables built in, colorful flags hanging from the low ceiling, and themed posters on the wall, this little place was always packed, especially late at night.

A group of kids our age was dancing by the entryway. My girlfriends and I got a table near them and, munching on tortilla chips with Coronas in our hands, started talking to them.

"Hey, where'd you guys go to school?"

"Uh, we went to school in Boston," one of them said.

That was code for "going to Harvard" if you didn't want to put someone off by the amazingness of going there.

My girlfriends and I rolled our eyes.

"Oh yeah? We went to school in New Haven," one of my friends replied.

They pulled up chairs. I was a little loopy from being out so late and felt completely disinhibited. The alcohol had worked its predictable magic and I was floating on my new life to come.

Charlie and I started chatting. And then we couldn't stop. What was his *story*? I wanted to know everything. He'd been recruited by Harvard for the football team, was the only child of a devout Catholic couple, and was currently unemployed.

And he was really good-looking. Tall, fabulous, lean, muscular body, warm brown eyes, a short beard, a big smile. I waved goodbye to the girls and talked to Charlie until 4:00 a.m. over pancakes at Florent, a nearby French diner. I was completely myself because it didn't matter. I would be going away in a couple of months.

So I went back to his studio apartment, a fourth-floor walk-up a few blocks away on Horatio Street. Later, he walked me downstairs and put me in a cab, kissing me on the street, giving me his phone number.

We started spending all our time together. Why not? He wasn't working and I'd given notice at Unilever. Our lease was up on our Upper West Side apartment, so Stacey and Sarah decided to move into a two-bedroom place downtown instead of trying to fill my room with a new third roommate. I was relieved no one would literally be taking my place.

But I was somewhat homeless for the end of summer and didn't want to live at my mom's apartment after years on my own. To be honest, I wanted to be with Charlie. Actually, he did sleep over in my childhood room once. That next morning he met my mother for the first time as she threw a load of whites into the dryer, wearing her bathrobe and slippers that scuffed against the floor as she shuffled in to get her coffee. That did *not* go over well.

I moved in with Charlie for the rest of the summer after knowing him only a couple of weeks. It offset the sadness I felt because Stacey and Sarah would be living together without me; this time they'd be unpacking boxes and rearranging furniture without my carpets and books and posters in the mix.

Charlie was different from the guys I had known. He drove a used, beat-up white van. He meditated every morning. He saw someone for "body work" and lived in the Meatpacking District before it was a cool thing. He ran marathons in his spare time and read spirituality books. A decade or two later, these would all be normal—in fact highly valued—attributes, but then it was a little out there.

One weekend, I brought Charlie to my mom's home in East Hampton. Years earlier, while I was in college, she'd gotten remarried to Howard, now my stepfather, a distinguished former coffee trader and partner at Goldman Sachs who could make friends with anyone as soon as he met them. Their wedding photos were actually in *Town & Country Elegant Weddings*.

"Howard Katz," he'd say, shaking hands with anyone new. His white hair was always just so, his shirts pressed and tucked in, round glasses on his friendly face. He is still called "the mayor" of his golf clubs, always up for sharing a root beer float or patting a friend on the back, saying, "What's new, babe?"

Howard complements my mom so well; he is calm, accepting, and even-keeled to balance out her occasional moods.

When Charlie and I were in the Hamptons, it felt like a scene out of a sitcom. We sat at the dining room table by the front door as everyone came home and commented on the van.

First Howard, after a day of golf.

"Hey, is the plumber here? What's with the van?"

A few minutes later, my brother, Teddy, walked in.

"Hey, saw the van. Did the power go out?"

I had to keep saying, "Actually, that's Charlie's van. This is Charlie!"

My mother was suspicious of this unemployed, bearded new paramour of mine.

"I don't know, Zib," she'd say, sighing, propped up against her piles of pillows, reading Laurie Colwin's *Family Happiness* in the late afternoon. "You don't even know him. I mean, who *is* this guy?"

"Mom, he went to Harvard."

I knew that for her, that fact alone would speak volumes and ratchet him higher on the social ladder. It apparently wasn't enough, as she'd shake her head at me and go back to her book.

Originally, I thought Charlie and I would spend the summer together and then break up when I went to business school in late August. But when August rolled around, I didn't want to break up. We were having fun! We had soulful, deep discussions about the universe. Why ruin it?

Over the summer, we'd gone to Rio de Janeiro in Brazil on a last-minute cheap online fare. We'd spent Sunday nights at Pastis with his crew of friends. I'd sprawl on his bed reading *Midwives* by Chris Bohjalian while he read spiritual tomes about energy work. We realized that we'd accidentally fallen in love.

———

Before I left the city, Stacey told me that sometimes she got nervous working at Marsh. She could see planes flying below her perch on the ninety-sixth floor of the North Tower of the World Trade Center. She worried about terrorist attacks after the bombing attempt a few years earlier.

"Don't be silly," I told her over Alaska rolls at an Upper West Side Japanese restaurant. "I bet there's even more security there than at other buildings after the last attempt. You're probably *more* safe."

She smiled and went back to her food.

"You're probably right, Zibs," she said.

And then the conversation moved on.

Soon after, Charlie and I went to my farewell dinner at Spice Market in the West Village with Stacey and Bryan (they had thankfully gotten back together) and Sarah and Sarah's boyfriend. It was the night before I left for school. Stacey arrived late, wearing a pantsuit from work with heels. The service at the restaurant was terrible, the din overpowering, and I didn't like my food. Nothing on the menu had even looked good to me.

It was the first—and last—time the six of us got together and we didn't exactly jell. The three boys were all so different. Our conversation was stilted, what I could even hear of it. I spent most of the dinner worrying about that awkwardness. What did it mean? Was it Charlie? I also felt like a seventh grader, worrying that Stacey and Sarah would be getting so much closer without me. I felt left out even though I was literally sitting between them.

After dinner we pushed our way out of the packed restaurant and posed for an awkward group picture on the cobblestones, our high heels making us as wobbly as circus performers on stilts.

I just wanted to go home and pass out in my little cocoon with Charlie; I was too focused on what was coming next for me. The big move to Boston. What to do about Charlie. A whole new scene. My fears about the academics.

So I hugged Stace and Sarah quickly, tightly, before walking away, looking over my shoulder as the four of them walked off in one direction while Charlie and I went in another.

———

The first two weeks at school were packed with welcome activities, classes, and schoolwork. I still needed alcohol to help me speak in social settings, so this onslaught of events tired my introverted soul immensely. I'd read *Note Found in a Bottle: My Life as a Drinker* by Susan Cheever, and could relate to her substance dependence, at least in social settings, but I couldn't really tackle it with all the events going on. I was quiet in all my classes, too scared to speak. At night, I'd wade through dozens of emails about ways to get involved at school. But my heart was still in New York City.

In those first two weeks of school, Stacey and I emailed often and had one long phone chat. I was nervous about the prospect of being "cold-called" in class and not prepared, so those first few days, I spent hours at my desk, rereading the cases and assigned texts, when I wasn't attending one of the eight million welcome events.

I didn't email or call Stace as much as I thought I would. I was just so busy—I was barely able to read a page or two of *Bridget Jones's Diary* by Helen Fielding at night before falling asleep with the book on my chest.

And guess who ended up in my class at business school? My ex-boyfriend Josh. Except I was there as his classmate, not his partner. Perhaps we were both always meant to be there together, one way or another.

O
2001–2003

Seven

Into Thin Air

A plane hit the World Trade Center!"
On September 11, 2001, I rushed down the hallway to class, passing a fellow student who was bent over one of the computer kiosks between the stadium-style classrooms. He was talking to a friend about some sort of collision.

I slowed down my pace as I tried to see the screen. What had he said? I assumed that a small plane had nipped its wing on the edge of the building. I couldn't see much and was about to be late for class, so I kept going, pulling out my cell phone and quickly calling Stace before popping into class.

"Hey, Stace, I heard about the plane. Everything okay?"

I thought back to her telling me about the planes she could see flying below from her office window.

Then I ducked into my classroom. I didn't think about it again.

When class ended, the hallway was pandemonium. A few girls ran by, crying. I heard one say, "My dad works there! I don't know where my dad is!"

"What's going on?" I asked someone passing by.

"Two planes! Two planes hit the towers!"

I stopped walking.

What? Two planes? I called Stacey again.

Voicemail.

"Head to Spangler!" someone yelled. "There's a TV!"

I followed the mob of students to the student center, carried by the tide. As I approached the back of the TV, I could see the faces of everyone else watching the screen, hands covering their mouths in shock, some sitting on the floor cross-legged, arms wrapped around each other. Others were crying. All were terrified.

"That's my old office!" someone said.

"I know so many people down there," another added.

I walked to where I could see the screen.

And gasped.

The buildings.

The smoke.

The holes.

The towers.

Stacey.

No no no no no no no.

I backed away from the crowd, silent, like a dog trying to get out of a tight spot, and ran upstairs. I burst out of the building, sprinting to my apartment. My heart was pounding. I couldn't breathe. I felt weak.

What if?

I had to get to a landline. My phone had stopped working. I had to call Stacey. Charlie. My family. Dashing past the beautiful brick buildings, the pristinely cut grass, the swarms of well-groomed students, I felt like I was in a dream. The bright-blue sky made the campus look postcard-worthy, as if I had been inserted into a picture from the admissions catalog. I ran, my school bag banging against my hip, reeling from the image of the gaping holes in the buildings. It was as if I'd seen a body with open bullet wounds. As a lifelong New Yorker, that bullet had hit me right where it hurt.

I raced through the doors of my apartment building, up the elevator, and down the hall to my new on-campus apartment, where a group of kids I didn't even know were congregated, along with my roommate, Amy. An old college friend, Steve, was there. He'd also been close to Stacey. No one spoke; all eyes were on the TV.

"My best friend works in the World Trade Center," I said, dropping my bag by the door. "I keep calling but I can't get through."

"Oh, Zibs," Steve said. "We're gonna reach Stace. Just keep calling."

I managed to get through to Stacey's mom, Martha.

"No word from Stace," she said coldly, in shock. "Bryan's looking for her."

I felt comforted knowing that Bryan was on the case and relieved, yet again, that they had gotten back together and even made plans to get engaged.

"I'll keep calling," I said. "I'm sure we'll hear from her soon."

We set up a call chain with friends and her family.

And then, as I dialed and dialed, the first tower fell.

One.

Then the other.

Time, suspended.

Life, stopping.

"Please be okay, please be okay," I whispered, my hands interlocked, my index fingers the steeple against my lips.

Steve and I hugged.

New classmates came and went.

I kept repeating, "My best friend works in the World Trade Center."

And I spoke to Sarah.

Sarah and I had gone to preschool and grade school together until her family moved to Chicago after first grade. I visited her every year after that for her school's Bazaarnival weekend and never lost touch. Years later, petite with long legs, beautiful thick blonde hair, a former debutante whose warmth made her beauty feel approachable, Sarah would be my maid of honor.

Sarah had yelled goodbye to Stace that morning over the sound of her hair dryer. Stacey had grabbed her Tod's tote bag and raced out the door. She must have click-clacked in her heels that day, turning heads with her bare, shapely legs, as she headed down into the subway station to get to the World Trade Center, the vibrant blue sky framing her as she descended out of sight. Sarah finished getting ready and headed to her advertising job.

Sarah was standing on Sixth Avenue, waiting for the light to change, when she looked up to see a plane flying way too low. The sound had caught her attention as it roared past. And as she crossed the street at 8:46 a.m. that day, surrounded by throngs of New Yorkers also rushing to work, she watched the plane until the moment it exploded into the center of Stacey's office building. People still bustled around her, not really noticing what had happened, as Sarah stared in horror.

She glanced at her watch and did the mental calculus. Stacey would've been there already. She would've had enough time to wait for the train, ride down to the World Trade Center, get off the subway, ride up the elevator to the ninety-sixth floor, and march down the hallway to her desk. She probably would've had time to boot up her computer, perhaps pick up the phone for her morning check-in with her mom. Perhaps that's why her mom's home phone had rung just once that morning, right as it happened. Sarah couldn't tell from the street right then, but the plane had hit exactly at Stacey's office. No one on that floor when the plane hit survived.

Sarah called Stacey repeatedly, standing on the street corner, as I called Stacey from the classroom hallway in Boston. Sarah didn't know what to do. She didn't want to be late for work, but what if something had happened to Stacey? She called her mom, waking her up in their family's new town house in Pacific Heights, San Francisco. And as she waited on the street—now joined by a few others who were slowing down to take in the scene—still talking to her mother, wondering if it would be okay to be late for work, she heard the second plane.

The roar. The shadow. The buzz.

And then: boom.

She watched it smash into the building. And she screamed. She screamed and screamed and started sprinting away from the subway, holding her phone, her heels hitting the concrete like staccato notes by a crazed pianist. She didn't stop until she got back into their apartment, closed the door behind her, and promptly vomited.

She sat in their apartment, willing the front door to swing open to reveal Stacey, imagining them hugging and comforting each other. But she sat alone, watching the news as the towers fell, one by one, until her boyfriend came over. Hours later, Sarah went up to Stacey's loft area and realized that Stacey had forgotten her phone at home that day. All those missed calls. Stacey, perhaps trapped, without a phone.

I asked Sarah for more details every time we spoke. What had Stace been wearing? Black pants with a black sweater. Exactly what time had she left? Had she eaten breakfast? Had she heard from Bryan? Sarah spoke to me from their kitchen table, unable to move the jean jacket Stace had casually tossed over one of the chairs. It stayed there until the day, weeks later, when I came with a group of Stacey's family and other close friends to pack up their apartment. While I was putting her unfinished business school applications into boxes, kicking myself again for not successfully persuading her to apply when I had, Stacey's younger sister, Laura, finally picked up the jean jacket. Stacey's favorite pearl earrings, family heirlooms, tumbled to the ground. We'd all been sure Stace had been wearing them.

That day, during my many hysterical calls with Sarah, I felt overwhelmed by guilt. I was the one who had introduced them. I was the one who suggested the three of us live together for that one year before I left for school. I was the one who had connected them, who had shown Sarah Stacey's bright light and infectious personality, had gotten her hooked like everyone else. And now, I had inadvertently created this trauma for Sarah by forging their friendship.

"I'm so sorry, Sar," I kept saying that day. "I'm so sorry." And then I would call her again. "Did she get back yet?"

"Not yet," she would say. Crying. Pacing. Watching.

———

Time slipped away. I paced. I tried calling. I spoke to other friends. Family. My brother, Teddy, a new college graduate working at a law firm, had been near the towers that morning and had seen people jumping. He'd walked all the way up to my mom's apartment on the Upper East Side covered in ash.

I finally reached him on the phone.

"Teds! Are you okay?"

"I'm okay. It's crazy out there. I walked all the way up here from Tribeca."

"Oh my gosh. Teds. I can't believe it."

"Yeah. When I got here, Mom asked me if I wanted a turkey sandwich. I don't think she's really processed this."

My mom had heard the news of the first plane hitting and then, not fully realizing the scope of the disaster, ran out to get her hair done as planned.

"Teds, Stacey works in the World Trade Center. Did you happen to see her down there?"

"Oh, Zib," he said, his voice filled with hurt. "Oh no. No. I didn't know."

"I'm sure she'll be fine. We just haven't heard from her yet."

"Zib, I was just down there. I wouldn't be so sure."

He sighed.

"It was really, really bad."

I didn't know what to do.

Later that night, the crowd in my apartment had dissipated. It was just my roommate, Amy, in her room with the door closed and me in mine. I sat at my desk, the same spot where I'd last spoken to Stacey. I perched in my desk chair and watched hours of footage of people jumping from the towers.

Jump.

Jump.

Jump.

Pause.

I zoomed in to find out if I could see Stacey's face pressed between the window slats of those high floors.

I paused the jumpers, freezing them in midair, as I leaned forward and scrutinized the pixels.

Ties, flowing up to the sky on upside-down men.

People holding hands, their bodies in odd angles as they fell.

I scanned all the pictures, looking for any signs. Could that be her shoe there, covered in ash? The one that had recently been discarded at our front door after we both got home from work and settled onto the living room couch to talk about our days?

I couldn't find a single trace of her. And yet, I still held out hope that she was somewhere, anywhere—perhaps wandering around the city with amnesia! That was how I reassured myself enough to fall asleep.

But she wasn't in any of the city hospitals. Bryan had checked. Hardly anyone was. The emergency rooms, poised to accept hundreds of victims, were empty.

———

The next day, I woke up and panicked. No news. I called Martha, Abby, Sarah, Rebecca. Stacey had just been down to Virginia for her interview at Darden, the business school at UVA, and had stayed with Rebecca, who was getting a PhD in clinical psychology. She'd returned home to New York only late the night before, on September 10.

That morning, she'd left Rebecca a note: "Reebs, I blew the fuse in the living room/office blowing my hair. I'm sorry! (You know how I just can't help 'blowing' everything.) I searched for the fuse box but in vain . . . Hope you had a great class! Love, S."

She'd gone to her interview and then flown back home alone. If only she'd stayed an extra day.

On September 12, classes at HBS were still on.

I shakily got dressed and somehow made it across the courtyard after grabbing my copy of *Creating Modern Capitalism*. But really, who cared? Baker Library, where my parents had met, gleamed at me a block away. I collapsed in my assigned seat. Silent.

The professor, a warm Indian man, started the lecture. He addressed what had happened with compassion and empathy and said that if any of us felt like we couldn't be in class that day, it was okay for us to leave. No penalty. I looked around. No one else was getting up.

I couldn't stay.

How could I sit there in class learning about leadership when the world was crumbling? I had to get back to the city. I had to find Stacey. I had to become an actual leader in real time. I packed up my cases and textbook, squeezed past the classmate next to me, and, with all eyes on me, walked out.

I sprinted back to the apartment to pack.

Even in a mad dash to leave school, I couldn't figure out what to pack and for how long. I stood in front of my closet and touched the hanger with my one black dress. Would I need it? How could I even think that way? I yanked it down, chose a few other outfits, grabbed a few books like *The Tipping Point* by Malcolm Gladwell and *White Teeth* by Zadie Smith. I called Stacey's mom in Connecticut to say I would stop by to see her on my way.

Her dad answered.

"Mr. Sanders, I'm on my way to visit. Is Martha there?"

He spoke slowly. Softly.

"Martha can't come to the phone. But yes, we'll be here."

The government had issued a no travel advisory. Only essential vehicles were supposed to be on the roads. But there I was, climbing into my little Saab in the empty garage on campus, firing up the engine.

Typically jam-packed I-95 was abandoned. It was just me. Driving. Alone with my thoughts. My fears. I hunched forward and grabbed the wheel tightly.

I listened to the news on the radio. I put my sunglasses on. Then took them off. Then on. Then on top of my head. I couldn't seem to decide on anything. I worried about getting lost. Usually, Stacey drove when we went to her house. I worried about all of it.

When I got to Stacey's house, Martha was sitting motionless at the kitchen table. Silent, blankly staring, comatose. I'd never been with Martha without Stace.

I sat down next to her.

"Martha?"

Nothing.

"Martha? I'm here." I took her hand. But I couldn't engage her or get her to talk. It was quiet in the house. Too quiet. She could barely look at me.

I didn't know what to do. What was the etiquette in a situation like this? I sat awkwardly beside her, just waiting. Finally, I said, "I'm going into the city now, Martha."

She finally looked my way.

"Please find her."

"I'll do everything I can."

———

I'll never know what happened to Stacey that day. Given the reconstructed timelines, the first plane hit soon after she arrived in the building. I always believed she must have been killed instantly while sitting at her desk because the first plane hit exactly at her floor. But a medium I spoke to recently, who knew many other things no one could possibly know, said that she believed Stacey had been in a stairwell with an older man, a coworker, when the tower collapsed. That she wasn't scared. Her mother spoke to a different medium who said that Stacey had just gotten off the elevator when the first plane hit.

I guess ultimately it doesn't matter.

No remains were ever found.

She just disappeared.

Into thin air.

———

Charlie could see the World Trade Center out of the one window in his walk-up. On September 11, he watched the smoke billowing upward, the gaping hole in the skyline a perfect frame above his head.

When I got to New York, the streets were empty except for police cars, sirens blaring. I went home first to see my mom and brother.

"I'm so sorry, Zib," my mom said, opening the door wide and trying to give me a hug.

Howard was next to her.

"Stacey's like a part of the family," Howard added.

"Zib. So sorry." Teddy hugged me.

I didn't want to be consoled.

"Guys, no, no, no. There's nothing to be sorry about. We're going to find her! I'm heading over to Bryan's to make more signs. I'm here now. I'll find her. I'll look everywhere."

They shook their heads.

I had to get out of there. Back to our friends who still had hope. I couldn't give up hope.

I drove down to Charlie's. On the way there I was stopped by tanks. He had to meet me on Fourteenth Street to show proof of residency and vouch that I was there with him. His view of the towers was scrubbed clean, like suds washed off a shower stall. Instead, smoke.

We went together to Sarah and Stacey's apartment. Everything was frozen in time. Sarah, normally completely laid-back, was hysterical. She hadn't slept.

"Zibs! You're back."

We held each other, crying.

"I keep throwing up. I don't know what to do. How to help. I keep waiting, but she doesn't come!"

"Let's head over to Bryan's. We'll get more signs to post!"

But as the three of us walked back to Bryan's Union Square apartment, Bryan let us know that he and other friends of Stacey's, Allie and Kathy, had posted all of them already. The picture he'd chosen for the sign was one I'd taken of her and Bryan from my college graduation party at my dad's house.

As it turned out, all those posters were just advertisements for the lives lost, faces staring out at the rest of us, who looked at them, shocked and traumatized, trying to make sense of the world. All would be documented in the *New York Times* series "Portraits of Grief."

I still can't believe we never found her.

Eight

EMPTY

I woke up at dawn at Charlie's in a postapocalyptic New York. I decided to go to the gym. A few days had passed but no luck. I was still in the city. I had to move. I couldn't sit still. While Charlie slept in, I walked down the silent streets of the West Village to Crunch gym. The air was musty and still smelled like stratospheric loss. Burning. I was one of only a handful of people there. As I checked in at the front desk, I realized that Stacey's membership would have to be cancelled. For days I'd held on to hope that she would turn up, until I couldn't convince myself anymore. There was no hope.

She was dead. I had to say that over and over in my head to really believe it. It seemed impossible. Dead.

"My best friend died in the towers," I told the receptionist. "She was a member here. Do you want her name?"

The receptionist shook her head.

"Most of our members aren't coming back."

We stood there, silent, our hands on our hearts, the whirring of treadmills our soundtrack of sudden death. We were enveloped in loss, spirits seemingly surrounding us, the last ones standing.

I ran, watching the news just a few blocks from the World Trade Center. Global news. Neighborhood news. My news.

I pushed the speed button up and up, running faster, racing against the truth.

Military tanks lumbered through intersections as I found my way home. Home to Horatio Street, where I'd climb the threadbare, creaky stairs to Charlie's place and try to figure out just how to do this new, horrific version of life.

Later, I sat on Charlie's floor with my laptop and waded through HBS emails. The running club was meeting at 7:00 a.m. Did I want to join? The section fleeces were in. What size did I need? Was I ready to order? Clubs, activities. Two friends with weddings were sending emails. One cancelled. The other kept her date. I changed my RSVP to no. No, I wouldn't be attending a wedding. No, I wouldn't be functioning.

Losing Stacey without proof, without a body, without a way to say goodbye and lay her to rest, meant a lack of finality and closure. I couldn't wrap my head around it. How could she have *disappeared*? But it wasn't just Stacey. It was the whole city suddenly on its knees. Reeling from absence.

When I eventually unpacked Stacey's clothes at her family's home, down in the basement with dust particles swirling in the sunlight, I found a single hair of hers on an old sweater packed in a box, mixed in with a bunch of my own clothes. I sat back and held the strand of hair up to the light. How could this be all that was left of her?

———

I started a new ritual. On Sunday nights, I would drive back up to school; sometimes Charlie would drop me off, sometimes he would stay on campus. And then Fridays I'd head back down to the city again. I'd hole up in Charlie's place except to pop in to the 24-hour deli across the street for a meal, snacks, or newspapers, where corn muffins wrapped in plastic balanced in piles by the checkout counter. Bagels were toasted and quickly encased in white butcher paper. I'd eat an entire carton of Ben & Jerry's Phish Food (frozen yogurt—as if that made it better) while reading *Flags of Our Fathers* by James Bradley. It felt like wartime.

Stacey's good friends and I planned the memorial service. We sat around Bryan's apartment and sifted through the pictures of her that we had all dumped on a coffee table, trying to choose the best one for the cover. In the glossy photos, Stacey was smiling, dancing, hugging, smooching the camera.

Only one of Stacey's other close friends wasn't there that evening. Her best friend from Andover, Abi, lived in Boston, and soon I would start seeing her at her art gallery on Newbury Street whenever we could. I'd met Abi many times over the years, including at one slumber party she hosted at her family's home. She often traveled from Brown, in nearby Providence, to visit Stace at school. I wonder if I'd been accepted at Brown like I wanted, maybe Abi and I would've become best friends there, and perhaps I would've met Stacey anyway, our paths destined to cross.

Horrifically, Abi's dad, Richard Ross, had been a passenger on the plane that hit Stacey's building. Sitting up front. Flying for work. The first plane. The one that crashed right into Stacey's floor. The two of them had burst into each other, mingling in exploded form forever. At the 9/11 Memorial now in downtown New York City, Stacey's name is etched in stone right next to Richard's.

Central Synagogue, a colossal, ornate building with wooden pews and breathtaking sky-high stained glass windows, was packed for Stacey's memorial service. Every pew taken. Standing room only. Charlie and I sat up front with Stacey's family and her other best friends—Abby, Rebecca, Sarah, Allie—as, one by one, we all clutched printouts of speeches and tottered toward the podium to share slices of Stacey. I spoke. It was the first of a series of eulogies I wrote that year. Having the gift of writing good memorial speeches isn't exactly one I coveted.

I'd written my speech sitting cross-legged on Charlie's floor; his studio was just big enough for the bed. Was it good enough? How could

I possibly summarize my relationship with Stacey? Our first year across the hall. Our second year in bunk beds, in a room as small as a jail cell. Living together in a three-bedroom apartment on Chapel Street for two more years. Standing together at graduation with our tassels swaying, holding our diplomas and beaming. On the Upper West Side, sitting under a Christmas tree. The High Holiday meals together at my mom's house. All the experiences. All the *time* together. Our trip to London to celebrate the millennium at a massive party of my father's, the two of us and a few other girlfriends in floor-length ball gowns on New Year's Eve, lounging on pink silk couches in the ladies' room at Claridge's Hotel.

I must have done a good job of summing her up because at the cheese-and-crackers reception that followed at the University Club, strangers formed a line to thank me, to hug me, to talk to me, even reaching out as I washed my hands at the bathroom sink to say how sorry they were.

Now my speech lives on in the 9/11 Memorial Museum, an actual recording, a video clip of me standing in front of that packed, broken crowd. Those memories. That time. Frozen. I found out about the clip from my stepmother, Christine, who had attended the opening of the museum and saw it when she was searching for Stacey's entry. (My dad had also gotten remarried.)

Years later, I found myself walking down Washington Street with a friend. We kept going south until we got to the memorial. I hadn't been ready to go when it opened, but that day was apparently the day. Outside, I stroked the letters in Stacey's name one by one, touching Richard Ross's as well, all of it flooding back like a giant wave crashing on an abandoned beach. And then, after descending endless escalators underground, I stood in the dark by the video screens, swiped on Stacey's name, and found myself. Right there. Speaking, moving, talking, gesturing, delivering the speech on a day that had previously been only a hazy memory. It felt like time travel. Two versions of me meeting in the depths of the earth, on the burial ground of my best friend and so many others, the scene of the slaughter. I started shaking, quaking, and told my friend, "We have to get out of here. Now."

I ran up the escalators and raced outside, gulping for air that never really came.

When *Good Grief* by Lolly Winston came out in 2005, I felt truly understood. A book about the loss of a spouse resonated more with me than anything else I'd read. It was divided into sections by the five stages of grief. It was about losing a soul mate.

I'd nuzzled into Charlie's strong arms on the night of the memorial, the maimed skyline above us, and cried.

———

The only way I knew how to cope was to write about what had happened. I wrote about it for the school newspaper, *The Harbus*, a few days after 9/11. In fact, I wrote column after column over the next few months, even though classmates looked at me with wide eyes and said, "Wow! You're so brave!" I didn't feel brave. I felt gutted.

And I read. I read my cases and coursework, yes, but I also read books to escape. I read books on grief. I read Anita Diamant's *The Red Tent, Tuesdays with Morrie* by Mitch Albom, Isabel Allende's *Daughter of Fortune*, and *Me Talk Pretty One Day* by David Sedaris. I gave books on grief to loved ones who grew concerned that my grief had been "going on too long" or thought that it was time for me to "get over it."

I ate with a vengeance. I'd bake a batch of cookies after class in my tiny kitchen, eat half of the dough, and then eat most of the cookies. One night, I was fueled by so much sugar that I couldn't stop pacing around the living room, pressing footprints into the plush beige carpet as if I were trampling a sponge.

My heart was thumping madly. I could almost hear it. I grabbed my sneakers from the pile of shoes in the bottom of my closet, laced up, grabbed my parka, and speed-walked down the long corridor, the faint sounds of various TV shows sneaking under students' doors. I passed the mailboxes that I dutifully checked each day and pushed open the institutional glass-front door.

A cold blast of air almost made me change my mind. I was alone in the courtyard at night, the whizzing noises of cars speeding along the Charles River off to the side. I started running, my hair whipping my face, my eyes watering. I passed brick buildings with dark classrooms. Dorms with students hunched over their cases, desk lights shining brightly through the windows. The student center. The gym in Shad Hall, from which a couple of students emerged, laughing.

I couldn't stop. The cookies. The sugar. The long night. The caseload. The pointlessness of all of it. The disappearance of an entire human being. Just like that.

I ran in circles, afraid to cross the bridge over to Cambridge so late at night, trotting around the tiny campus, the rawness of the river mixing with my racing pulse, until I was too breathless to continue and stumbled back to my tiny apartment. The vertical plastic shades that shimmied to the beat of the heater greeted me.

———

Each week, I revved up my car in the freezing cold and drove across the river to a residential area in Cambridge. I double-parked (terribly, always) and walked up the steps to a worn, beloved, covered porch.

Dr. O'Brien met me at the door, smiling.

"Come on up, Zibby."

A trauma therapist, Dr. O'Brien would sit me down on the soft green couch in her home, flowers and framed photos covering the quaint apartment, and settle across from me on an upholstered armchair, adjusting a pillow behind her back.

"How was the week?"

I counted down to our therapy sessions.

Her kind, patient eyes.

Her thoughtful, compassionate smile.

The way she could reframe my experiences and help me cope with the everyday aftermath of what had happened.

"Not great," I would say.

Without any family in town, I also thought of Dr. O'Brien as a surrogate mother, comforting me when I was in the depths of despair. My mother, though, had flown up to be with me on Yom Kippur, one of the only people on the flight from New York to Boston so soon after all airplanes were grounded. I dropped my tissues in a painted waste-basket on my way out, biding my time until I could come back again.

Nine

One L

The crippling shyness was back.

When I wasn't in New York, I would sit in my classroom at HBS on the second floor of Aldrich Hall, fully prepared for the day's classes, and watch as the conversation ping-ponged from one student to another.

At the start of the semester, our professors had given us a clear directive: never speak out of turn. Our comments must build on the ones that came before. It was imperative that we follow the weaving dialogues wherever they went. Like joining the horah dance at a wedding, we had to wait for the right moment and seamlessly slide in without disrupting the flow.

But it didn't matter if we were raising our hands or not. The professors could call on us to answer any questions at any time: a "cold call." I would sit there in my assigned front-row seat in what students called the "worm deck" and turn my head to and fro, listening as my classmates discussed finance, accounting, marketing, operations. I just couldn't seem to produce and share thoughts on the requisite timetable.

And yet, most of our grade was based on in-class participation. I walked into every class determined to speak that day, only to walk back out an hour-plus later, my mouth dry. Occasionally, I'd raise my hand to add something, but then the conversation would surge past, rendering my comment moot or irrelevant. I couldn't seem to keep thoughts in my head long enough and would jot key terms down on the top of my cases so I'd remember them.

I'd always been able to quickly grasp and retain material, spending hours in college in the art history building, memorizing hundreds of paintings, artists, dates, and locations for finals. But I wasn't excelling academically at business school. I was barely getting by. While I understood the cases I read, I just didn't have that much to offer in class discussion. I wasn't learning finance and accounting very well. I needed a textbook, not a debate, to master the net present value calculations. And honestly, I barely cared.

Every day in class, I watched the conversation zing around me, students from Japan, Mexico, the UK, France, South America, Turkey, Nigeria, and New Jersey adding their insights in a carefully orchestrated chorus.

I knew that my loss was making my brain more muddled, but still. Should I not have been admitted? Had I been accepted because my dad had attended and was a donor? Did everyone assume that? I was sure they all thought I was simply a legacy admit despite my strong GMAT scores, relevant work experience, academic success in college, and desire to achieve.

While I feared the same when I got into Yale, I could prove myself with my grades and school involvement. At business school, I lacked the chops to master the participation-focused grading system, especially with my brain short-circuiting in trauma mode.

I wanted to be back in New York, not huddling with new acquaintances as we bundled up and froze crossing over the bridge into Cambridge for section events, the blast of cool wind whipping off the Charles River lodging in my bones.

And then I failed my accounting exam. Failed. I hadn't failed anything since seventh grade, when I came back to school after being out sick for two weeks with the chicken pox followed by the flu and took a test about the Trojan War, which I'd completely missed learning about.

My big red F confirmed that I didn't belong at school. I didn't want to go into marketing anymore. I didn't want to start a business. I wanted to get under the covers and never come out.

I couldn't run to the closest bathroom fast enough. I dodged packs of students in the crowded hallways, my eyes welling up, until I locked myself in a stall and unleashed the torrent of tears. I was failing in every way. Everything was ruined. I didn't belong. I couldn't take it.

I called my dad from the bathroom. His assistant got him out of a meeting.

"Yes, Zib?"

Crying so hard I could barely talk, I wailed, "I failed my accounting exam, Dad. I failed! I'm dropping out of school. I can't do this!"

He chuckled good-naturedly.

"Oh, Zib," he said. "I think I failed accounting, too."

"Seriously, Dad. I can't be here anymore!"

"Calm down," he said. "It's one test, Zib. You know, in the real world you don't need to know accounting that well. You just need to *hire* great accountants. I was never that good with numbers. I could barely do the math!"

"Dad . . ."

"Let's get you some extra help. Can you meet with the teacher?"

"I don't want to get extra help. I want to come home. I don't want to be here anymore!"

Someone flushed in the stall next to me.

"Don't make any rash decisions, Zib. You're not in a good emotional place. You tend to act impulsively based on your feelings, but your feelings may change. Do you want me to have my accountants give you a call and help you understand what you're confused about? Maybe I can send someone up there."

"Dad, no! I'm already embarrassed enough."

"Zib, it's one test. It doesn't matter. All it means is that you didn't understand the material. It's not a judgment on how smart you are. So let's help you understand the material."

"Dad, I'm dropping out."

"Zib, don't. You'll always regret it."

Another flush in the bathroom.

"I gotta go. I love you."

"Chin up, Zib. Remember, nobody likes accounting!"

He chuckled again.

"Bye, Dad."

I hung up the phone, wiped my eyes, and ignored his advice. I was dropping out. I walked straight to the administration building, padded up the plushly carpeted stairs, holding the glossy wood banister, oil paintings of men hanging from the walls, and landed in the dean's office.

A jolly-looking man with wavy white hair, blue eyes, and a kind smile sat behind the desk. I would come to know him very well.

"How can I help you?"

"I'm here to drop out of school."

He came out from behind his desk and walked over to me, compassion in his eyes, an arm extended.

"Let's talk about it," he said. "Come, sit down."

He patiently listened as I cried, and then, instead of mandating that I stay, simply said, "Well, let's see if there's a way we can make things a little easier for you. How about that?"

He took me under his wing and helped me navigate academics and my grief. We made a plan: he got me an accounting tutor, encouraged me to see someone at the health center about my depression, lauded every article I published in the school paper—where I eventually became the Features and Viewpoints editor—and read my essay about 9/11 in front of the whole school. Without Steve Nelson, I wouldn't have made it.

———

"My study group wants to know if you want to join. We have room."

A new sectionmate, Sam, and I were walking back to our on-campus apartments after class.

I didn't want to join an early-morning study group. But I was still in danger of failing. Almost every other student at HBS was part of a study group that worked on assignments together, met for an hour before class, finalized financial models, and analyzed the details. It was part of the HBS experience and highly recommended. But it was optional. Perhaps had I been in a different frame of mind I would've joined one and headed off to the Spangler student center each morning for breakfast and study group, to prep for the day's cases like my roommate and everyone else. But at the time, I just thought: "Why on earth would I do *that*?" Wake up an hour earlier to discuss the assignments that I could quickly do myself the night before or, since there was nothing to physically hand in, not do them at all?! I spent my time reading for pleasure and writing. Breakfast was for drinking coffee and reading the newspapers, not navigating Excel.

"Hmm, could I just come to check it out? Make sure it makes sense?"

"Sure."

The next morning, Sam and I walked into the cafeteria, which was packed with groups of students hovering over cases and spreadsheets, laptops open. I was immediately overwhelmed. I can't stand crowds. I get anxious and panicky, and I always want to turn and run home. An ideal day for me is staying in bed with a laptop, writing and reading. Hundreds of students all talking about academic formulas I didn't understand? No, thanks.

Sam's group was welcoming and lovely, but the conversation among them about the finance concepts went too quickly. I was already lost but too embarrassed to admit it. What if they found out how stupid I was?

I felt like I was carrying around the most toxic secret, one that would alienate me from the high-powered, confident kids.

At the end of breakfast, we all stood up to head over to class.

"You guys are so nice to invite me," I said, grabbing my tote bag. "But I think I'm going to skip being in a study group after all."

Instead, Sam offered to help me one-on-one. I felt comfortable enough with him to admit when I was lost as he explained the issues in finance. Another classmate also started helping me in accounting. I was in a free fall, but Section B '03 was standing beneath me, ready with a net.

———

My book club at business school was also a saving grace.

Our group was made up of fellow students and "partners" (significant others of students). Our group included a consultant from Chicago, an investment banker who would go on to run a stationery business, a partner who became a top Google employee, a poet, and an economist who now works in a government think tank. At school, we took turns hosting, discussing novels and memoirs over goblets of red wine as snow fell outside. Sometimes we drank hot chocolate.

I had a favorite pair of wool pants I used to wear, charcoal gray with a few white pinstripes, wide-legged and cuffed, with a clasp, not a button. I'd throw on a pink sweater set and boots and brave the cold, clutching my book. I measured time between book club meetings, relishing escapist reads like *Atonement* by Ian McEwan, *Shopgirl* by Steve Martin, *The Greatest Generation* by Tom Brokaw, Amy Tan's *The Bonesetter's Daughter*, *Seabiscuit* by Laura Hillenbrand, *French Lessons* by Peter Mayle. I got under the covers in bed, my cases tucked away in my bag for the next day, and lost myself in stories.

Other students complained about coursework. Yes, I did the required case reading, but I read the assigned material at the gym on the elliptical machine or exercise bike. It really wasn't that much reading; each case was about twenty pages. Typically, we had three cases a night, plus questions to prepare. But sixty pages for me wasn't a big deal. At college, I'd taken comparative literature classes and plowed through complex texts. Three cases? Please.

And yes, I did the homework, but for the first time in my life, I was doing the bare minimum. Unlike college, where I worked so hard I had to go to the ER one night with the stomach ulcer I'd given myself from stress. Unlike high school, where I stayed up late studying and working, only taking breaks for *90210* and *Melrose Place*.

Good enough would have to do. Not everything could be perfect.

It was one of the most important lessons I learned at business school.

Ten

Good Grief

My grandpa Joe adjusted the hospital bed to see us better. Just before spring break in 2002, my dad's dad had been diagnosed with a virulent form of leukemia. Our extended family had flown down to Sarasota to say goodbye. Huddled, holding his hand for the last time with my aunts, uncles, and cousins, marveling at his bravery and charm even in the face of death, I struggled. I couldn't bear to see my own dad and his younger brothers gutted, crying. The final closing of "the store." Grandma Arline, ever stoic, pushed through it, bossing him around until the end.

"Joe, sit up, the grandkids are here."

He smiled up at her, happily complying.

"I'm a lucky guy," he told us, only welling up with tears once. "I love you all so much. What a life. Great life. I can't complain. Right, Arl?"

He looked up at my grandmother.

"Right, Joe."

I hugged him tight, the bed railing jutting into my stomach, before leaving for good.

My grandfather passed away just as I got back to school.

After the funeral in Philadelphia, I snuck upstairs to sit in my father's childhood bedroom, where I stared at the many trophies, framed certificates, and black-and-white photos of my dad from track meets. I tried to imagine what it had felt like to grow up in this house, in this room, with this bedspread. I thought about the summer he dislocated his shoulder and spent months in that same bed. The room was a shrine to my dad—nothing had moved an inch since he left for college in 1965.

Charlie was the only one tall enough to wear my grandfather's clothes. They had the same build: six feet tall, lean, fit. Grandma Arline gave him most of the clothes.

"You might as well," she said, going through their closet matter-of-factly, my grandfather's work shoes lined up with shoehorns in each one. "Everyone else in this family is too short."

We drove home from that service, blazers and pants and coats bobbing behind us, a soul stirring in the backseat.

———

Somehow I made it through the end of the school year. I'd gotten a job that summer in brand planning at Young & Rubicam, an advertising position I'd wanted since junior year of college. I felt shaky every time I entered the office building in New York, imagining how I would escape if it caught on fire, trying to find the stairways, on edge listening for that whirring sound of the airplane. I'd read *A Big Life (in Advertising)* by Mary Wells Lawrence and *Ogilvy on Advertising* by David Ogilvy.

Charlie and I rented an apartment together across the street from his studio, one with a bit more room for me, too.

A week into the internship, my new office phone rang. I'd given the number to only my parents and Charlie for emergencies.

"Zib, it's Mom. I have some bad news."

Howard's firstborn son, Adam, my stepbrother—and the father of three little boys—had died suddenly from an accidental lethal drug interaction. He had been spending a few weeks in LA after separating from his wife, Julie. His sister had found him.

I'd known Adam for almost ten years. We'd taken family vacations together, sharing a home in Aspen for a week of skiing when Julie was pregnant with their second child. I'd babysat their son Zack. Julie was so cool—how she wore Adam's button-down shirts from his job as a Wall Street trader over a pair of black leggings instead of maternity clothes. They were the model couple, an example of what I wanted when I got married. Adam, a shorter, squatter replica of Howard with the same voice, same charm, same warm and affable personality, was always the person I hoped my mother would seat me next to at holiday dinners, our names written in calligraphy on place cards perched on the starched white tablecloth at our long dining room table.

Now Adam was gone.

How could this be?

My cab pulled up to the awning of my mom and Howard's apartment and my childhood doorman, Vincent, came out to open the door. He was wearing his standard uniform of a suit, matching cap, and white gloves.

"Hello, Miss Elizabeth!"

(He is literally the only one to ever call me that.)

"Hi, Vincent." I could barely hold back the tears.

"Go right on up. Your mother is home."

I walked across the marble lobby floor and into the mahogany elevator, steeling myself. Poor Howard. Oh my gosh. Poor Howard.

The same aroma as always greeted me, the mix of a heady scented candle and wood chips. I walked through the rounded foyer, under the tiered crystal chandelier, through the wood-floor kitchen, and into the family room where Howard could always be found watching sports on TV in his slippers.

And that's where he was. Watching baseball on the couch, my mom reading the newspaper on the chair next to him as if it was any other day.

I sat beside him and gave him a hug.

"Howard, I'm so sorry," I said, starting to cry.

"Thanks, kid," he said, still watching the screen. "It's a terrible thing. Terrible."

My mother got up and took me into the other room by the arm, whispering, "He just wants to watch TV. He won't talk about it."

A few nights later, we gathered in the apartment with family and friends, the dining room table now a buffet, Adam's place card tucked away in a drawer with the others. Another black dress. I'd invited a few new business school friends who were working in the city for the summer. We chatted somberly, unsure of what to say.

At the memorial service at Frank Campbell on the Upper East Side, I sat up front with my mom and Teddy and watched as Adam's three small young boys filtered in, wearing matching blazers, to say goodbye to their dad. The image haunts me even now, although the boys are in their twenties and all over six feet tall and thriving.

———

At the end of the summer, right before heading back to my second year of business school, I visited my mom and Howard in East Hampton. It was my twenty-sixth birthday. Gagy called early; she never missed a birthday. Every time we talked we'd trade book recommendations.

I picked up the house phone in the kitchen, staring at the clock on the oven.

"Hi, pussycat," Gagy said, a little quietly.

"Hi, Gagy!"

"Happy birthday, dear heart."

"Aw, thanks, Gagy! How are you?"

"Well, not so good."

"Not so good? Why?"

She sighed. Waiting.

"Well . . . I didn't want to tell you this on your birthday, but Papa Kal died early this morning."

She started crying.

Papa Kal. The rabbi. The guitar. The big hugs. Her soul mate.

I covered my mouth. A snarling, angry alligator pit formed in my stomach.

"What?" I gasped.

"I kept hoping he would wait until tomorrow so he didn't ruin your big day."

"Gagy! Oh please. Are you kidding? My birthday isn't even important. I didn't know he was that sick. Are you okay?"

"It's just been the two of us and the hospice nurse for the past few weeks. You know he's been ill for quite a while now."

"I know, Gagy, but—"

"The end was quick. I know he would've wanted you to celebrate today and enjoy. He loved you so much, you know. You were his special Lizzy-belle."

She sniffled.

"I know, Gagy. He loved *you* so much."

"I know."

We both cried.

"You reading anything good?" she asked through her tears.

The next morning, we flew out to Dayton, Ohio.

On the way to Papa Kal's funeral, Charlie felt sick on the plane. As we got up so that he could head to the bathroom, he unexpectedly stumbled forward and then crashed to the floor, where he lay flat in the aisle, unconscious. Doctors were paged by the pilots. We pulled him into the galley kitchen, where he woke up on his own and started drinking water. When we landed, I wheeled him out to the taxi in a wheelchair, my new laptop—which of course I forgot—hanging from the handlebars. Charlie ended up being fine after some sort of virus but spent the funeral trip in bed at my grandparents' house. As my dad would say, "Never a dull moment, Zib!"

———

Trauma sniffed me out again the following month, like a German shepherd searching a crowded airport. This time it was a close friend from high school.

I first met Avery outside of Central Park the summer after ninth grade, right after I got home from my trip to France. She was a close friend of a classmate of mine; they'd both gone to Spence, and now she was back, after a year of boarding school, to join our class. Avery wore cutoff jeans and a faded yellow polo shirt, a cool rope necklace, Tretorns, no socks. She chain-smoked, flicking ash with the top of her thumb. She was painfully thin, but beautiful, with her freckly face, blue eyes, thick dark-brown hair, slightly crooked nose, high cheekbones, and big smile.

Although I had a group of friends already, Avery was different. The two of us just clicked, not as part of my larger friend group, but as a twosome on the side. She made me laugh. And she was so smart.

We spent the rest of that summer in the Hamptons together, going to the beach, playing tennis, having sleepovers. That fall, we started walking to school and taking the bus together in the mornings, which we did every school day for three years, sometimes taking cabs home late at night after our tennis team matches or lacrosse practice. We both loved to read and would pass books back and forth across the bed as we lay on our stomachs, our bare feet waving in the air, the Park Avenue taxis sighing on their way downtown.

Soon, we were having dinner at each other's houses even on school nights. We studied together and made mixtapes. The following summer, we went on a tennis tour through Europe. We played in tournaments from Belgium to Denmark. I typically lost in the first round and ended up eating french fries served in white paper cones while sitting on splintery wooden benches on the sidelines, watching my peers. She'd get a little further but sometimes threw the matches to hang out with me.

Avery dared me to do things just out of my comfort zone. When the group of us went to Wimbledon, she begged me to leave early with her and take a London cab back to the hotel before the rest of the group. I followed. I did whatever she said. Up to a point.

As high school went on, Avery zoomed past my comfort zone and headed to her own dangerous territory.

Our senior year, during a sleepover at my house when my mother was out of town, we concocted a plan to skip school the next day. Why not? It was the only time I would ever break a rule like this. The next morning, we said goodbye to my nanny, Mary, got dressed for school, and then, instead of walking north up Park Avenue and then across town to school, we veered south, went to my mom's garage, and asked the attendant to please bring up my mom's car.

And he did.

We called the school office pretending to be our mothers.

Avery had her driver's license already, so she drove. We blasted Z100 and WPLJ and headed out to the Hamptons for a glorious, blue-sky Tuesday. On an empty stretch of the Long Island Expressway, she was pushing ninety miles per hour. I put my feet on the dashboard as she smoked out the window. Rebels that we were, all we did in East Hampton was go out to lunch at Babette's, a cute restaurant in town, and then go bowling, before driving all the way back to the city in time for the school play that night.

While that day marked the most rebellious thing I *ever* did, for Avery, it seemed to be a turning point. I didn't know it then, but mental illness was descending on her like a fly that she tried batting away but couldn't. Her anorexia and bulimia flared up again. She started doing cocaine. She started selling her mother's jewelry to buy drugs.

Eventually, Avery had to be hospitalized in an inpatient unit for eating disorders. My dad drove me up to her treatment center in Westchester, where they inexplicably let her leave with us to go to Rye Playland for a few hours. I repeatedly consulted the school psychologist—panicked, hopeless, frantic—for help on how to reel her back in. How could I help? Was Avery going to die?

As a naive high school senior, I also selfishly felt abandoned, traded for the kids she was suddenly hanging out with, the students who did drugs on the weekends. I wrote her letters, called her parents, and helped her find psychiatrists for her previously untreated borderline personality disorder.

Being a genius, Avery had applied early and gotten into Princeton. The admissions team didn't know what had happened to her since her mom had affixed the admissions letter with a magnet to their refrigerator. But she was so smart that despite the chaos going on in her brain, she could excel at her coursework in both high school and college.

Perhaps it's no wonder that when I went to college, I majored in psychology with a specialty in eating disorders.

She and I had visited Princeton together, with her dad before he passed away and she truly descended into darkness. We sat in the grass that day and watched the students weave in and out of beautiful buildings; we gossiped about friends and talked about the boys we'd smooched the night before. She fell in love with Princeton on the spot.

Throughout college, Avery was in and out of treatment centers, but she still managed to graduate. When I moved back to New York from LA, she'd just gotten out of the hospital again and was living in a run-down apartment in the East Village with male roommates I didn't even know. I went down to visit her, even though the day of our plan, I couldn't reach her on the phone to confirm. She'd recently run away from her latest treatment center, a habit that had cost her family so much money they'd had to turn to a "tough love" approach. They weren't helping her anymore. She didn't want to be helped. But I didn't want to give up.

I took my mom's car service to get down to her neighborhood. Emaciated druggies wandered around in front of her building's entrance. My driver asked, "Here? You sure?"

Avery's roommate finally buzzed me in. I walked up four flights of filthy stairs, food wrappers, needles, and condoms everywhere. Avery was asleep in her bed in a dark-red room. She wasn't moving. I tried waking her up and she wouldn't rouse, no matter how hard I shook her. Was she alive? I checked her breathing. Yes. I had started to call her mother when Avery finally woke up. She barely recognized me.

"It's me, Ave!" I said. "It's Zibby. Let me get you out of bed."

She pulled up the covers.

"Come on," I said, nudging her. "Are you okay?"

It took ages, but she finally sat up, groggy.

"What are you doing here?"

"I moved back to New York!"

"Where were you?"

"I was in LA for two years, remember?"

She shook her head.

"I need a cigarette," she said.

She climbed out of bed. She must have weighed eighty pounds. I followed her onto the building's roof, where she lit up.

"How did you get back here?" she asked, more lucid.

"What do you mean? I just moved. I hired a moving company and packed up my apartment and came back. I'm rooming with my friend from college, Stacey. Remember her? We all had brunch a few years ago. And my friend Sarah. I know you know her, too. Blonde? Really pretty?"

Avery nodded.

"Oh yeah," she said. "They're nice."

I pictured the photo I had on my bulletin board of Avery, Stacey, Sarah, Abby, Rebecca, and me standing on Sixty-Third and Park afterward, dressed up on a bright spring afternoon, arms around each other.

She inhaled and exhaled smoke up to the bleak sky.

"Ave, I'm worried about you," I said. "You can't live like this. You don't seem well. Can I find you a doctor? Someone to help you? You need help."

She looked at me and started crying, flicking her cigarette ash with the top of her thumbnail as she always had.

"How do you do all this?" she asked. "How can you just move across the country? It seems so hard. I can't do anything."

I leaned over and took her tiny birdlike frame in my arms.

"I'm back now. I'm going to help more. I didn't know things had gotten so bad."

She pulled back.

"It's okay," she said. "I'll be okay."

By the end of the visit, I was calling doctors at Mount Sinai Hospital to help. I wrote down all the appointment details for her and the doctors' names. I even called her mom while I was there to let her know about the appointments, how badly Avery was doing. And then I hugged her again and left.

She never showed up for the appointments.

The next month, Avery disappeared. I got a frantic call from our mutual friend, Serena, who had to use her political clout to hire a detective to find her.

"She's missing? What do you mean she's missing?"

Serena's voice crackled.

"We're going to find her."

For the next few days, I was a mess. Where could she be? How would the detective locate her?

We found out, shockingly, that she was by the Santa Monica pier in California, all the way across the country, homeless, not taking her meds, deep into drug addiction. Serena got her off the streets and into another treatment center in a dramatic middle-of-the-night rescue mission. Avery, the gorgeous, funny, brilliant girl, wasting away on the streets? It was impossible. What could I do?

When I left for business school, Avery was starting to get outpatient treatment again in New York City. In my own grief and haze post-9/11,

I only intermittently checked in with Avery and her mom, seeing her just once that summer.

In early September of my second year at business school, just after the anniversary of 9/11, I was leaving a restaurant in Cambridge with a group of friends when my phone rang. I stopped on the sidewalk to answer it, asking my friends to wait just a sec.

"Zibby, it's Kalen," she said.

Avery's older sister. She had never called me before.

"Hi, Kalen."

"I'm sorry to tell you this . . . but Avery took her own life today."

No.

No.

No.

"What? No! Are you sure?"

"I'm sorry. I know how good a friend you were to her. I know how much she loved you."

That morning in New York, Avery had thrown herself in front of an approaching subway car.

I still have the mixtapes.

The pictures of us arm in arm. Playing tennis. At the beach. Watching *90210*. Taking our trip to Europe. I can still see us leaving Wimbledon. Studying for the SATs. Sitting at her kitchen table while her mom made us fresh tortellini. Lying on her bed together, listening to Green Day. Planning our senior retreat. Shopping for John Fluevog shoes in the Village. Wandering around East Hampton town. Reading *The Catcher in the Rye* by J. D. Salinger (which made Joanna Rakoff's memoir *My Salinger Year* even more poignant) and *A Farewell to Arms* by Ernest Hemingway side by side. Going to the movies. Sitting in Central Park. That day at Princeton. Bowling. All the normal high school things.

Then, a subway.

How could I not have saved her?

———

The group I was with on the street in Cambridge that night gathered around me. They all knew about Stacey, of course. Now I had to tell them about Avery.

My friends walked me back to my apartment and sat with me in the living room while I cried. Soon I would be planning yet another memorial service, coordinating speakers, printing the program with Avery's gorgeous picture on it in the basement copy store of the student center, a few feet away from the TV screen where I'd watched the towers smolder. Another group of mourning young friends, now just twenty-six.

What else could possibly happen?

Of course, it wasn't happening *to me* at all. I was a bystander as other bright souls went out like lightbulbs that popped. At Avery's service, so unlike Stacey's, held at Serena's apartment in the city with just a few friends, I read yet another funeral speech I'd written, this one just for our group.

I told Avery to look for Stacey up there and to save me a seat between them.

Avery. Stacey. Grandpa Joe. Papa Kal. Adam Katz.

When my old friend Steve, who had sat beside me on the couch waiting for Stacey to call on 9/11, asked Charlie how I was doing during one of his visits to campus, Charlie just sighed and said, "People have to stop dying, man."

I'll be forever grateful to Charlie (not his real name) for the strength with which he carried me through that time. His patience. His arms to cry in. His empathy. His deep sensitivity and compassion. His love. Our love. It was an unforgettable time.

———

During this period of intense tragedy, I found myself at my intern-ship, preparing a presentation for Pepperidge Farm cookies. As I moved around PowerPoint slides, sitting silently in my corporate office, I real-ized I just couldn't do it.

All the loss. All the grief.

My fingers were poised over the keyboard. And I stopped. If I was going to die at my desk like I believed Stacey had and if my life could end at any moment, then I had better be doing something that involved my whole self.

All of me.

I would finish my internship, but after that, anything else I chose to spend my time on professionally would have to be a labor of love.

Worth it.

Worth dying for.

Worth living for.

It took me a while to find it, but through books, I found my way.

Eleven

HEARTBURN

I kept denying it. I didn't want to admit that my relationship with Charlie was slowly ending. I was starting to get clues but I would just turn up the volume, determined not to hear the messages my heart was emitting in not-so-subtle ways. I was noticing other guys, one in particular. I didn't want to call Charlie back as quickly. I was reluctant to visit him where he had started business school himself and miss out on campus parties. I was starting to come out of my shell a bit at HBS, just in time for graduation.

On the bus to Charlie's school, I would stare out the window at long stretches of highway and wonder if I was doing the right thing. Charlie's and my deep conversations hadn't stopped. But he wanted to raise his kids Catholic while I wanted them to be Jewish. He wanted to live in Boston while I wanted to be in New York. We were both very sensitive and would simultaneously fall into bouts of sadness. Instead of taking turns, often we would descend together, with no one left to lift either of us out of our moods. I knew we were reaching a natural end point but I hated the thought of breaking up with him. Charlie had been there for me through my five losses, sitting by my side at memorial service after memorial service. Now that school was ending, was it fair to say goodbye?

The cocktail of meds dreamed up by the health center hadn't been very effective. One antidepressant, an antianxiety pill, then a second antidepressant on top of those. Later, when I consulted with an acclaimed New York psychiatrist, he was horrified to hear what I'd been taking and quickly got me on a better combination.

As much as I cared for Charlie, part of me knew at this point that we were bringing each other down, two people trying to save each other in the deep end, grasping tightly, yet both sinking. I needed a buoyant partner, an antidote to my deep darkness. Someone permanently wearing a life jacket, someone who could laugh and move on easily, unlike me. I knew that was what I needed. And Charlie needed for me to let him go and live his own life, devoid of all my trauma. Not that he admitted or consciously knew that. I wanted him to live his life unencumbered by my *mishigas*, as my grandmother called it.

———

The week before graduation, a group of us rented an enormous house on Key Biscayne in Miami for one last hurrah. Dozens of soon-to-be-employed overachievers going for a farewell voyage by the sea? Why not? Between student loans, signing bonuses, credit card max outs, and pure hubris, we all justified the trip as essential, a necessary period to the paragraphs of our MBA experience. Others, more calculating, justified it as a networking expense, an investment in their post-MBA contact infrastructure.

I was just celebrating getting out of there. All I wanted was to be back in the city and with the people I'd known forever. People who really got me. Who had known and loved Stacey. I'd ended up with some lasting friendships and many warm relationships at HBS, but it had always felt like I was wearing the wrong cut of jeans, a pair that should have looked good on me, but just didn't fit quite right. I wanted to rip them off, toss them on a nearby armchair, and never put them on again, except every so often to marvel that I'd worn them for so long.

I decided to take a year off after graduation to write a book and process what had happened. All that loss. I would work from home and tell my story. I would set it at HBS. I read *One L* by Scott Turow to see if I could model it after that.

On that Miami trip at the end of school, one of my classmates booked an afternoon of waterskiing. Finally, I could exhibit the random talent I had for slalom waterskiing, honed during six years of sleepaway camp in Maine.

I bobbed up and down with the foamy life jacket riding up under my chin. The water was freezing as I thrashed around to grab the handle. The boat puttered farther away, pulling the line taut as I firmly held on. Thumbs-up.

I was off. One of my classmates was driving the boat. How had he gotten permission for that? Why didn't we have a captain? Who knows? I watched the tiny speck of him at the helm as I got ready to stand up. The other guys on the boat were all drinking already and yelling, "Go, Zibs!" as the engine revved.

Zhoom. My one ski cut through the water slowly as the boat sped up. I wobbled side to side until—ahhhh!

I was up, skidding on the sea. It was just like I remembered. The cool air slapped my face like I was in a car wash of wind. The loud roar of the boat. The pinprick sight of the boat passengers in the distance, waving their arms but silenced by the motor. The sky, endless and enveloping as I surfed the tide, bouncing up and down.

Typically, the boat goes at a reasonable speed: fast enough to make sure the skier's rope doesn't go slack, but not so fast that it creates excessive turbulence in the water. My friend at the helm hadn't gotten the memo. As I watched the crowd cheer, I could feel the boat speeding up. A little too fast. Definitely too fast. The water became roller coaster choppy. I geared up to cross over the wake where the water might be calmer, away from the propulsion just behind the boat.

Smack! I slammed against the water at full speed, my side slicing into the water, my body cracking. I couldn't breathe as I tried to get upright, and when I did, I saw my watch, the heavy silver one my mom had given me as a graduation present, floating in the water in front of me. The ski bobbed up and down. I grabbed them both and gasped. My side was killing me.

"That was awesome!" one of the guys said.

"Want to go again?"

"What a wipeout!"

I shook my head, gasping, treading water.

"My side! I have to stop."

Two guys reached over the side of the boat and pulled me out of the water, where I inelegantly flopped like a freshly caught fish. I landed on the sticky white seat that clung to my bathing suit, and tried to decide what to do. One guy said, "Drink it off, Zibs!" and handed me a beer.

Back at school the next week, I was packing up my bedroom in the cottage-cheese-ceilinged, super-plush-carpeted on-campus apartment where I'd survived the past two years. Where I'd watched my world change on TV. Where I'd mourned Stacey and so many others. Where I'd fallen apart.

And I sneezed.

Crack!

Just like that, the rib I'd injured waterskiing snapped. I dropped to my knees and clutched my side. I literally couldn't breathe. My roommate wasn't home and I couldn't move. I just sat there, immobile, until I worked up the energy to crawl to my phone and call a friend.

I simply whispered, "Can't breathe. Can't talk. Rib! Hospital!"

The X-rays showed the fracture. I wasn't allowed to lift anything for the next three weeks to let it mend on its own, despite my plans to pack up, move out, travel to LA for a girls' trip, and then move back to New York.

The fact that I left Boston broken, unable to even pick up my own belongings, was fitting.

I couldn't carry one more thing.

I had to leave so I could start to heal.

K

2003–2009

Twelve

SEX AND THE CITY

It all went down on East Twelfth Street. After graduation, Sarah and I moved into a light-filled two-bedroom apartment between Fifth and University, without our third roommate this time. Stacey's other good friend, Allie, happened to live in the same building. We were trying to restart our lives.

Every morning, I worked out in the nearby New York Sports Club. Then I'd eat a quick breakfast, shower, blow-dry my hair, get dressed nicely, and scooch into my desk to begin writing. I worked at the same Ethan Allen wooden desk and hutch I'd had since college, the one my mother and I shopped for in the giant showroom one rainy summer day, the one she encouraged me to invest in because good quality would last longer.

I cracked open my laptop and, with the cursor blinking, grabbed the stack of pages I'd written the day before to see where to pick up the thread. I was writing about what had happened during business school. To Stacey. To my family and friends. The ripples of loss.

I worked on that book full-time—dressed up and keeping regular hours—for nine months. While my former classmates were off being associates at consulting and private equity firms, powerhouse companies like American Express and Chanel, I was alone in a room with a keyboard, but I was elsewhere in my imagination.

Sarah and I watched *Sex and the City* together every Sunday night, often with other girlfriends piled on our couches. Then each Monday morning, I would turn on my laptop and create an alternate world for myself on the page. I started by copying and pasting every email or letter or essay or document I had about Stacey or my time at school into one giant file. I showed that "draft" to an editor. Written in diary form, it was more of a source document than a book.

The editor called me afterward to discuss what I had sent her. She was disgusted by it.

"What even *is* this?" she asked. "How can I even edit this? This isn't a book. I don't even know what this is."

I held the phone to my ear, speechless.

"Well," I said, "I wanted to show what I went through by—"

"Right, well, really this is a bunch of emails from a whiny girl. All those emails with your parents? I mean, all you do is complain. Why? I don't even get it. I don't know why you wasted my time with this."

"It's about my five losses and—"

"Look, if you want me to help you with something, write it as a book first. Make it fiction. Try it another way. But this? This is just nothing."

I was so stunned and hurt that all I could say was, "Okay, thank you."

And I sat there, on my bed by myself, and sobbed. It took weeks before I could drum up the courage to sit down and write again.

For my birthday that year, a close friend "gave" me a role as an extra in an episode of *Sex and the City*, which was amazing. I was going to be on the set of the most popular show ever, the show based on the book, which I was going back and reading between show episodes. I also read *The Between Boyfriends Book* by Cindy Chupack, another show writer.

Commanded to show up at Lotus, a club in the Meatpacking District, in my coolest "going out" clothes, I reported for "work" in a sleeveless black tank, big dangly earrings, a red skirt, and strappy heels. The wardrobe team took one look at me and nixed my outfit. They beckoned me into the back room, where they had me try on a pair of pants reminiscent of those worn by Tweedledee and Tweedledum. Standing alone in a makeshift dressing room wearing those blooming pants, I thought, "There is no way I'm going on TV in this outfit. I'm not even leaving this stall."

Once I opened the door, the team agreed and gave me a more forgiving skirt to wear. For the next four hours, I sat on a sticky leather couch reading *Life of Pi* by Yann Martel while surreptitiously trying to spot Carrie or Charlotte.

This was what being on TV was like? Seriously?

Finally, someone boomed, "Extras! All extras! Head upstairs!"

I jumped up and filed into the club while stage managers positioned us around the dance floor and bar. That took another hour. I was starting to get sleepy. And then in waltzed Smith Jerrod and Samantha. Gah! I tried to stay cool in my random dance floor stance instead of craning my neck to watch the scene across the room. And then, two minutes later, they waltzed out again and it was over.

Months later, a gaggle of girlfriends gathered in our apartment. When the scene came on, I hopped off the couch and stood right next to the TV. And then . . . nothing. Where was I? Not even in the background?

"Wait, rewind it!" I told Sarah, who was holding the remote.

On the third rewind, I shouted, "There! Stop!"

If I looked closely, I could see the upper right quadrant of my forehead. I took a picture of the screen and then my friends took pictures of me standing next to the paused screenshot of my forehead slice as we laughed.

In the "day job" of finishing my book, I'd decided to turn my own story into a fictitious narrative. Every twenty pages or so, I would drop off stacks of printed pages at my business school classmate Lea Carpenter's apartment on the Upper East Side, leaving them in a large manila envelope with her doorman. She had written a novel, *Eleven Days*, that was stunning and beautiful and would come out soon. She would send me edits, which I'd come and pick up.

One chapter a day. I'd take breaks only to eat. I didn't stop to email or make calls.

I can see myself from above: my quaint, downtown, verdant neighborhood, me at the desk typing, the birds chirping in the trees that tickled my window, the bed perfectly made behind me, the chapters lined up in piles on the cool wood floor, the outline partially crossed off, my fingers flying on the keys.

On the days when Lea was reading my drafts, I would write for magazines. I was taking a writing class at The New School one night a week with a fantastic, no-bullshit, New York teaching legend, Sue Shapiro, who wrote *Five Men Who Broke My Heart* and *Lighting Up*.

Some of the things Sue taught me have shaped my approach to life. For every article pitch, she said, make a list of the ten to fifteen publications you think would be a good fit for your story. Fill in the chart with the publication name, editor name, and contact info. Start with the first one and work your way down. Don't pitch multiple places at once. Give each place a week or so. When they say no, it's no big deal. Just go down to the next name on the list and immediately send the piece out again. If you're lucky you'll sell it before you get to the bottom of the list. If you don't, either it wasn't good or you're trying the wrong places, so rewrite or add new places to the list. She also assigned brilliant essays by women warriors like Cheryl Strayed, who would go on to write *Wild*, designed to make us think, learn, and feel.

Sue taught me that rejection isn't personal. She explained life from the editor's point of view—how overwhelmed with submissions they are, how they sort through pitches. She challenged us to research the publications extensively before pitching. Even now, if I'm pitching a piece to, say, *Parents* magazine, I make sure to read the previous six months of issues. There's nothing worse than pitching a piece just like one that's already running. Sue then dared us by saying that she would take out to dinner anyone who could sell a piece for $1,000.

I liked that challenge.

Within weeks of starting Sue's class, I sold a personal essay to *Modern Bride* called "Confessions of a Bad Guest," which they ran on the back page of the magazine along with my picture. I'd unknowingly showed up to a wedding wearing the same dress as all the bridesmaids. I also sold a piece to a local free newspaper about learning how to roast a chicken. Then I sent a blind email to an unknown editor at *Shape* magazine with a list of twelve different topics I wanted to write about. I was working out daily then, twice a week with a trainer named Aldo, and had the gym on my mind. The *Shape* editor actually called me on the phone, thanked me for the pitches, and said, "Well, how about we start with these six." Six! I tried to play it cool and said, "Sure, that works," before getting off the phone and screaming in excitement.

I sold an essay to *Quest*, a high-end Upper East Side rag, about how much I missed the corn muffins at Barefoot Contessa in East Hampton and how sad I was that the store had recently closed. Little did I know that Ina Garten, a friend of my mom's from the shop, would go on to become the international media star she is today.

Whenever I take a bite of a buttery corn muffin, my go-to comfort food, I think of Barefoot and Ina, the smell of freshly roasted coffee in that corner market, the bustle of shoppers picking over the glass cases of delectable prepared foods, and how writing about that particular loss, the store's closing, masked the gaping hole of Stacey's loss.

———

If only all the loss in my life had translated to a loss on the scale. My clothes weren't fitting anymore despite my frequent workouts. I had to try something new. A close girlfriend of mine was having success with Weight Watchers. I'd actually never tried it, but boy, had I tried everything else. Atkins. Carbohydrate Addicts. South Beach. The Zone. Everything. My bookshelves were full of every diet book on the market.

I headed across the street early one morning to try it out.

An elderly woman with wavy white hair and a Long Island smoker's accent named Lenore introduced herself as my "leader." Every Wednesday morning from that first day on, I would grab my small, folded Weight Watchers member booklet and head to the nearby church to be weighed in. A "receptionist," a woman who had had success with the program, would take my booklet from across the desk, write the day's date, and then say, "Go ahead, please."

I'd take off my shoes, my jewelry, my watch, anything that could weigh an ounce, and step on the cool, ridged scale. If I had bare feet, I'd put a paper towel down first. Did that weigh anything? I'd stand there awkwardly while the receptionist looked at the number from behind the desk, a number I couldn't see, and then said, "You can step down, dear."

Sometimes I asked the receptionist right away: "Am I down?"

Other days, I'd preempt her with "Don't tell me."

She recorded my weight by hand in the little booklet and handed it back to me. Sometimes she'd say, "You're down .4!" or "You're down two weeks in a row!" Other times she'd say, "You're up a bit this week. Were you expecting that?"

Occasionally, I'd burst into tears and say, "But I did everything right!"

After each weigh-in, I was handed the pamphlet of the week, which focused on a particular topic and included a recipe. Then, holding my papers and all of my assorted discarded vestments, I walked over to the seating area to find a folding chair for the meeting. Before the meeting started, I would analyze my weight trends, sometimes pulling out my weekly "tracker," into which I recorded every "BLT" (bite, lick, and taste).

I was given twenty points a day to allocate to all the foods I ate, plus thirty-five bonus "points" each week. Each point was roughly sixty calories. I wasn't eating much and I was working out daily. It started to work. Really work. Week after week, I would come back to the church and step up on that scale.

After Lenore led the group meeting on a particular topic, giving us a "tool" like positive self-talk and then providing a forum for women to commiserate about their struggles, she asked if there were any celebrations.

One day I couldn't contain myself. I raised my hand.

"Yes, dear?" Lenore asked, as the group looked over at me.

"I lost five pounds," I said sheepishly.

"Congratulations!" Lenore said. Everyone in the room applauded, looking at me and smiling. I think I was the only person in the room under age seventy. Lenore walked over to me, her buxom chest bouncing under her floral scarf, and handed me a bright-red bookmark that said, "I lost five pounds" and had a heart on it. I laughed and thanked her. When I got back to my apartment, I displayed it proudly on the fridge before making my one-point egg white omelet.

I could do this. Forget the diets that I'd started at age nine. This would be different.

Just as I typed my pages each day, I'd also count my points in my tracker. I was marking time and accomplishments in small increments. Crossing off chapters as I wrote them in my book outline. Crossing out bonus points as I spent them. Crossing out publications as I went through the list of article pitches. It wasn't school, but it was a system, a way to structure the world that made sense enough for me to get through each day.

And I read. I read books about grief and loss, manuals like Elisabeth Kübler-Ross's five stages of grief, memoirs like Dani Shapiro's *Slow*

Motion. I wanted to read about how people survived loss. I read Mitch Albom's *The Five People You Meet in Heaven*, lost myself in *The Da Vinci Code* by Dan Brown, fell into *The Kite Runner* by Khaled Hosseini, found a kindred spirit in *Reading Lolita in Tehran* by Azar Nafisi, felt haunted by the girls in Alice Sebold's *The Lovely Bones*.

By the end of the year, I'd lost all twenty pounds. Before, I'd been blasting myself with sugar hits to take the edge off my grief: any baked goods would do, especially heavily frosted cupcakes and muffins.

Now I was shedding the protective layer I'd added to shield my fragile soul from sadness. I started to get carried away. I could *really* do this! Something was working! By turning every food into a quantifiable entity, I no longer had to debate if I "should" or "shouldn't" eat something. I could eat half a cupcake as long as I counted the points. Nothing was off the table. It was all just a game. How many zero-point foods could I eat to keep myself full enough for the next low-points meal I would eat? Not only did I hit my ten percent weight loss target, which resulted in Lenore hugging me and all the ladies giving me a standing ovation, but I became a lifetime member, which meant I hit my goal weight and stayed within two pounds of it for six consecutive weeks. (Once you became a lifetime member, meetings were free for the rest of your life.)

It suddenly all seemed so easy to me. Something I'd struggled with since I was nine years old was finally fixed! There had been a solution all this time! I was so excited and enthusiastic about the program that I decided to start working at Weight Watchers so I could help other people the way I'd been helped. As was required, I started by working part-time as a receptionist, weighing people in.

Now I was the one saying, "You can step on."

I made friendships at the scale, repeat customers who would wait in my line just so they could see me. I would beam at members who lost, share concern if they'd gained, and celebrate their accomplishments while selling products to them and marking up their little booklets. The low-points products were chock-full of chemicals, but we didn't care! We were losing weight! Members loaded up on bars and shakes, their arms brimming with what they hoped would allow them to meet their goals each week. After every meeting, I would do the math manually and reconcile all the member fees and product sales, restocking the shelves with boxes containing more goodies.

Occasionally, I wondered what on earth I was doing. There I was, a freshly minted Harvard MBA, and I was working as a receptionist, stocking shelves. A few times, someone I knew would come in to be weighed.

"Zibby?"

I was mortified and proud at the same time.

Within a few months, I was promoted to meeting leader. Now I could be the Lenore of the group.

Over time, I became disillusioned—I met several leaders who would talk badly about their members after meetings, leaders who ran from meeting to meeting, hawking products for more pay in commissions, grumbling afterward about the "lazy women who will just never lose weight, but they better keep coming in!" I was so horrified that there were leaders who thought that. It was like finding out my psychologist laughed at me over dinner after every session.

I was given plum assignments, like the "at work" meetings where I would go into companies like Avon and do their lunchtime meeting in a corporate boardroom. I was working at multiple centers around the city: Upper East Side, Upper West Side, Midtown West. I carried around my giant flip chart and hiked all over the city, up and down on the subway, walking, moving.

My boss even secretly gave me some private clients in a hush-hush arrangement for a select few who were willing to pay exorbitant amounts to have a leader come to them. Instead of $11.95 a meeting, these clients paid $750 for five sessions. Five sessions with me! I kept a portion of that money, but Weight Watchers kept most. I didn't even care. I was making a difference. Harvard Business School's oft-repeated mission is to educate leaders to make a difference in the world. Well, Joan on East Sixty-Ninth Street was losing weight with me and feeling better about herself. Did that count?

Meanwhile, I couldn't stop losing weight and was obsessing about food. My mastery had gone too far. I'd always been a size 8–10; that's where my body naturally wants to be. One afternoon, I went shopping with my mother, who I'd also persuaded to come to my meetings. Instead of the typical dressing room drama about how nothing fit, I could wear anything I wanted. Everything looked good because everything fit! The size 2 was loose. Could it really be the right label? A size 2 was hanging low and loose on my hips? My mother was elated. She'd been trying to help me lose weight since I was in fourth grade, when she had me write down my daily calories and measure half a cup of orange juice before I drank it. In retaliation, I'd started buying Hershey's Kisses across the street from my grade school and hiding them under my bed to eat in secret. Suddenly, I'd done it. Never mind the fact that by then I'd stopped getting my period. Never mind that my hair was falling out. That I could never get warm. That I felt sick all the time.

Soon trips to various doctors' offices made their way onto my calendar. Ob/gyn. Endocrinologist. Nutritionist. I was still technically a healthy weight according to Weight Watchers, although I was the lowest allowable weight for my height. No doctors, aside from one who was trying to help bolster my fertility, suggested that my eating might have something to do with my health. The artificial sweeteners. The chemicals. The food substitutes that were lower points, like shakes and bars. My daily snack of cucumbers sprinkled with Splenda. While my actual weight seemed "normal" for my body, it was way, way too low for me. My systems were starting to shut down. "Idiopathic," they called it. "Unknown cause."

But I knew the cause.

It was seductive, the power of controlling my body, my intake. I looked good. I had never been thin before. In reality, I had an undiagnosed eating disorder. I thought about food nonstop. I cried when I was denied access to egg whites and had to eat real eggs, which, by the way, had only two points each. I would plan every meal out days ahead of time. If a restaurant's menu wasn't online, I would call ahead and request to hear specials. No oil, no butter, dressing on the side. I weighed every ounce of chicken. I measured one cup of grapes. If I went to a wedding in, say, Santa Barbara, I would drive twenty minutes to the nearest gym to fit in my morning workout. I wouldn't allow myself a single day off.

Instead of anyone in my life seeing this behavior as problematic, everyone applauded me for it, just like the ladies in Lenore's lineup. Only my brother took me aside and pointed out that writing down every single thing I ate and eating, say, seven almonds, was just weird.

When I look back at pictures from then, yes, I can see how thin I was. But I also see a lonely young woman racked by loss and grief, trying to exert some control over a terrifying world by measuring and weighing every ounce of sustenance. I see a woman desperate for approval and validation. I see a girl living with only one of her two former roommates, filling that empty room with the chatter of points, the click-clack of computer keys. I don't see happiness in the picture. Even my smile looked strained. I may have been thin, but I didn't look good.

Now, I weigh more than I did when I started Weight Watchers that early Wednesday morning. But I'm happy. My face looks full, soft, and sometimes pretty. My eyes twinkle. My hair is thick and healthy. I'm rarely cold, although of course now I've started getting night sweats as I enter middle age.

I'm not thin. But I'm healthy. Strong. Where my body wants to be.

I wrote an article for *Redbook* magazine years ago in which I interviewed Gagy, Grandma Arline, and all their lady friends about their bodies. I even designed a little survey to correlate a past history of eating disorders and other mental health conditions with food attitudes, reminiscent of my psychology studies in college. Many of the women still weighed themselves daily. It turned out that many elderly women still struggled with unresolved eating issues. Age alone healed nothing. Many still beat themselves up when they ate, say, a piece of chocolate cake, carting themselves off to Curves to repent.

I couldn't let that be me. I had to get it under control or I would spend my whole life obsessing and hating myself. I had to be grateful for the abundance in my life and for every day I got to spend here on earth. I mean, really, wasn't *that* the "point"?

Thirteen

ON WRITING

It was time to find a literary agent. I wanted to sell my book, which I was calling *Off Balance*—how I felt during that time. I printed off six copies on loose-leaf paper and kept each one in its own white cardboard box, ready for publishers. Many agents passed, but Sara Crowe, a friend of a friend, took it on. I told everyone I knew. Had I been on social media then, I would've posted about it. My lifelong dream of being a published author was just ahead. Attainable. Possible. I couldn't even sleep, I was so excited.

Sara sent off copies to six publishers.

And then we waited.

And waited.

And waited.

After each rejection, she would call me, sounding both guilty and discouraged.

"Sorry, Zibby," she'd say. "We've had another pass."

I was standing in my mother's kitchen in New York when I heard the final news. I'd called Sara on the landline, the one my mom used to phone in her grocery order every day for delivery from Butterfield Market.

"Our last publisher responded," Sara reported. "They really liked all the parts about the friendship and your writing, but they think it's too soon for a 9/11 novel. It's too fresh. Too raw. They want to know if you'd consider rewriting it so that the friend dies in a car accident instead."

"But the book is *about* 9/11," I said.

"I know."

"So how could I possibly do that? It would take away the whole point."

"Maybe you want to just think about the idea?"

"No, sorry," I said. "I can't do that. I just can't."

"Okay," Sara said slowly. "Well then, it looks like we're at the end of the list. It just doesn't look like it's going to sell. I'm sorry, Zibby."

"So that's it?"

"It's too soon in the market for this book. Everyone has passed for the same reason. I don't think it's worth continuing to submit."

Silence.

She was giving up. We were giving up. After spending almost two years of my life on this project, a very public and risky endeavor, I had failed.

I'd failed Stacey. Stacey's family. My friends. Myself.

I hung up the phone and sank onto the scratchy kitchen chair. I put my head in my hands and cried. It was a giant, obscene, public failure.

I should've been working in advertising, I thought. Why did I decide not to go back to Young & Rubicam after my summer internship? Instead, I was a receptionist with a failed book, two degrees, and probably an eating disorder. I was a professional disaster. And everyone I loved kept dying.

All I wanted to do was talk to Stacey about it. But I couldn't. And all our mutual friends were also grieving. I felt so low I wasn't sure how I would ever go on. Yet wallowing wasn't an option. I was still leading meetings all over the city. My private clients were waiting. They didn't care if I sold a book or not. They cared only if I showed up smiling and encouraging at their front door. If I could give them the warmth and motivation at the scale.

And what about the book? The story? All those pages? All those trips uptown to drop off sections. The time I spent rewriting them. The effort. All those hundreds of thousands of words? What a waste! I'd always believed in my writing. Not that I was any sort of genius, but I was decent enough. I understood words. I could hear them as I wrote. I could adjust to make them sound better on the fly. I knew I could communicate my innermost feelings through writing in a way that would help people. Why couldn't I sell this book?

My agent called me back a few weeks later. Would I be interested in a ghostwriting project? She knew a fitness trainer, Ashley Borden, and a fashion designer, Paige Adams-Geller, of Paige Premium Denim, who wanted to write a book using their knowledge about how to work out and dress well for any body type while bringing in their own battles with eating disorders.

Um, yes. I didn't know how to do it, but I would figure it out. After Avery's recent suicide and all her time in inpatient units for eating disorders, I knew this next project was right for me. I could help other people and try to succeed where I'd failed her. And I could learn more about the writing process.

I met Sara in her office the next day at Trident Media Group. It was smaller than I expected, just a few desks and a couple of employees. I thought a literary agency would look glamorous. This was just a regular office with some books strewn about, papers everywhere. We huddled in front of her giant desktop computer as she taught me how to write a nonfiction book proposal. She logged on to Publishers Marketplace and showed me how to look for competitive titles, how to see what similar projects sold for, and how to learn what was coming out soon. Every section of the proposal was important. Together that day, we crafted *Your Perfect Fit: What to Wear to Show Off Your Assets, What to Do to*

Tone Up Your Trouble Spots. Then we showed it to Paige and Ashley. They loved it.

I wasn't emotionally invested in the project this time. It wasn't my blood, sweat, and tears on the page, but that was perfect. It felt like I'd just had my heart broken, and now, instead of getting in a new committed relationship, I was just dating. This book felt like a dinner downtown, a blind date that was going well, not a deep, amorous relationship. It was my rebound book.

In the middle of all this, I had met someone and recently gotten married. And now I wanted to start having kids. When I wasn't reading and researching health and fitness books like *Skinny Bitch* by Rory Freedman and Kim Barnouin, or reading the *Hungry Girl* blog, I was inhaling any books on fertility I could find so I could get pregnant ASAP. *The Fertility Diet* by Jorge Chavarro and Walter Willett hadn't come out yet, but I quickly realized I had to stop using ten packets of Splenda a day. All the chemicals in those Weight Watchers shakes and bars couldn't be helping either. One doctor I consulted told me I needed to gain weight. Me! Ha! After all those years of never being able to lose weight.

The book proposal sold to McGraw-Hill just as I found out I was pregnant with twins.

I was elated. We'd have a published project! Ashley and Paige had even been generous enough to allow my name to be on the cover along with a "with" attribution, which was a big deal for a debut ghostwriter.

The manuscript's due date and the babies' due date were the same.

Fourteen

Your Perfect Fit

The bleeding wouldn't stop. I was twelve weeks pregnant, living in a town house off Second Avenue. Was something happening to my babies? Was I okay? What was wrong? I'd already gotten so attached to the tiny humans growing inside me, I'd named them. I'd had monogrammed sweaters made. They were real people to me. What if?

I rushed to the high-risk OB's office, praying.

Please let the babies be okay.

Please let the babies be okay.

I couldn't stand it. Had I done something wrong? Maybe I'd caused this by walking too much the day before? Too much stress?

Luckily, after the doctor's exam, I found out the twins were okay, but to prevent more complications I was instructed to go on bed rest. No getting up. No stairs. Nothing.

"For how long?" I asked.

"We'll see you back here in a month," my doctor said. "We can reassess then."

"A month," I repeated. I couldn't sit still for five minutes. But with all that primal fear coursing through my veins, I knew there wasn't anything I wouldn't do to make sure the kids were okay. Mothering starts long before babies arrive.

Bed-bound, I hired a lovely woman named Tenzin to help clean our home, take care of my new bulldog puppy, Mabel, and do other things around the house that I couldn't. She was only slightly older than I was and had two little boys of her own. She'd left her nine brothers and sisters and her parents behind in Tibet and channeled all her kindhearted energy and love into making sure I was okay and the babies would be all right.

I know that it's always complicated, a relationship that is also a job, but I do believe that love can transcend almost anything, particularly a "professional" relationship. I mean, how do we cut off our whole selves and only give a sliver? After fifteen years together now, Tenzin and I have weathered all storms together, tag-teaming child care, wordlessly knowing who is doing what next. I love Tenzin. And she is a part of our family. Full stop.

My mother had a similar bond with our family's housekeeper, Connie. Connie had worked for us since I was eleven years old, just in time to help pack up my father's belongings that day he moved out. She came to the US when she was nineteen and somehow landed in our home. With no other family in the United States, she'd become a part of ours.

Now that I was almost thirty years old and on bed rest, Connie came over to help after Tenzin left in the evening, bringing me new maternity clothes from the Gap since I couldn't shop. Connie would make roast chicken in my kitchen, yelling up, "Hey, Zeeb! You want roasted potatoes?"

Of course I'd shout, "Yes!"

When Connie got married a few years later, my twins were the ring bearer and flower girl. My mother and Howard walked Connie down the aisle. We celebrated her becoming an American citizen. Years later, my son locked himself in my mom's bedroom one day, and Connie climbed out the window of the room next door and shimmied along the Juliet balcony hovering ten floors over Park Avenue to save him. All with a laugh and a smile. She brought that same energy and helpfulness to taking care of me when I couldn't do anything myself except grow babies.

———

Every day during the book-writing process in my last six months of pregnancy, I would interview either Paige or Ashley. Propped up in bed, my belly growing bigger every day, I would hold the landline phone between my shoulder and ear while I typed with both hands. My goal was to write the book in their voices. Of course it was. After my book was rejected, I assumed no one wanted to hear my own voice. I didn't even know what it was anymore. The blank page, which had always been a safe space for me to express my innermost feelings, had betrayed me.

Ghostwriting was the perfect career solution. It was what I'd been trying to do with my novel anyway: write about ghosts.

My body grew like a Macy's Day float being blown up the night before the parade. Every part of my body filled with fluid until I was a caricature of myself. Even my nose was puffy and misshapen. The liquid my body produced to support the two little ones inside was so vast in quantity that, weeks after giving birth, when it had evaporated, I exclaimed in surprise at seeing my ankle bones again.

As I grew, the book also took shape.

I was stuck inside. Isolated. Working all day. Fighting against time. Talking to authors. Ushering a book into the world. I read constantly when I wasn't watching *American Idol*. I read *Momzillas* by Jill Kargman, *Three Junes* by Julia Glass, and *What to Expect When You're Expecting* by Heidi Murkoff. Occasionally, friends or family would come visit, but I really remember only Connie and Tenzin from those long days on bed rest, which lasted from weeks 12 to 24 and then again from week 32 until I delivered. Thanks to them, I gave birth to the book and my twins, right on time.

Later, when the book came out, I hosted a little book party at home. My twin babies made a surprise appearance. I gave away books and signed a few for close friends. A giant poster of the book cover perched on the mantel. Women, and a few men, gathered around to discuss the book, eat, drink, and be merry.

I loved every minute of that book party. It wasn't the book I'd set out to write, but it's the one that sold. Either way, I'd become a published ghostwriter. And a mom.

Fifteen

SIPPY CUPS ARE NOT FOR CHARDONNAY

My agent emailed soon after the twins were born. Would I be interested in writing another book, this time for a well-known fitness duo with a studio nearby in the Hamptons? Yes! Sara set up a meeting. I was living at my mom and Howard's house for the summer, nursing my twins around the clock. An hour to myself to drive to Bridgehampton and back? I couldn't wait for the silence of the drive.

And yet, as soon as I got in the car, I panicked. I started to hyperventilate. I debated turning around and racing home. What if something happened? What if my mom dropped one of the babies? Or they had a seizure? Or there was an earthquake and I couldn't get back to them? I was having a panic attack. Logically, I knew nothing would happen. Emotionally, I felt like I was going into battle, all senses on high alert, my mom protectionism like a Care Bears light beam shooting from my tummy.

I took the meeting and sped home. I decided I couldn't be apart from the kids again. I couldn't work outside the home. Not yet. No meetings. I wasn't ready. Perhaps this was just a bout of separation anxiety, but I didn't fight it. If I was going to stay home, though, I was going to ace that job. I would be all in. I wouldn't miss a meal, a walk, a bath-time, a bedtime, an activity, a book.

"Zib, you're driving yourself nuts," my mother would say as I raced around frantically, trying to do absolutely everything. My mother thought my parenting style was crazy, from the breastfeeding to the overinvolvement in the kids' lives.

"Let me help! Let Tenzin help! You don't have to do every single preschool pickup! You don't have to give every single bath. Benign neglect, Zib. Benign. Neglect."

I "neglected" her advice.

"Things were different when I was little, Mom," I'd say dismissively. "You just don't understand what it's like now."

To further bolster my stay-at-home-mom success potential, I taught myself how to cook new things, making my way through the Barefoot Contessa cookbooks and hosting small dinner parties.

I would master my kids' nap and eating schedules, which I had typed out, double-spaced, down to the minute, and taped to the fridge. I would attend every story-time at various bookstores. I would be at all the Little Maestros music classes, not missing a single cue to further enhance the learning experience. No, I wouldn't sit there gossiping with a mom I knew. I had to stand the baby up! I had to shake that rattle! Wave that parachute!

And I refused to give one child more attention than the other. Sometimes I would run back and forth across the street between my daughter's Broadway Babies acting class and my son's Kids in Sports session multiple times. In one hour! I didn't want to miss a minute.

And yet, my mission backfired. Depression draped itself around my shoulders like a long-lost friend coming by for a cup of coffee as I was racing out the door: inconvenient yet familiar.

I knew I should be happy. I had beautiful twins. I was living in a ridiculously large four-story town house in the heart of Manhattan, a place where every time I opened the front door I would run into someone I knew. I didn't have to worry about money, thanks to my dad and my family's generous and thoughtful strategic planning, although during the downturn of 2007–2008 I panicked and started selling my purses and jewelry on consignment, cut expenses drastically, and tried to find every single document showing exactly what assets I still had as my overall wealth plummeted.

Yes, I was a privileged, Upper East Side, stay-at-home mom. And I knew it. I knew how lucky I was every single minute. But I couldn't enjoy any of it. Why couldn't I just go to spinning class, get my nails done, and meet girlfriends for lunch every day like some of the other uptown ladies did? I wasn't taking advantage of any of the perks of the "job." When my kids napped, I dealt with emails and wrote instead. I took my mom job too seriously, putting extreme pressure on myself, as if I'd get in trouble if I took lunch "off."

To feel more emotionally fulfilled, I got involved with several nonprofits. I'd been a tutor at the East Harlem Tutorial Program, so I jumped in to help their junior board organize some fundraising events. I enlisted fellow MBAs to build the audience for Lincoln Center Theater's productions. I organized several fundraisers for the Young Friends of Mount Sinai and helped them innovate and attract new members. I sat on the junior board of the American Museum of Natural History and the Young Lions of the New York Public Library.

The library was my favorite. About twenty of us in our twenties and thirties huddled around a giant mahogany boardroom table in the private trustees room on the second floor of New York's most iconic institution to plan the Young Lions programming each year. The wood walls had oil paintings of library leaders and elaborate painted ceilings. We listened with rapt attention to up-and-coming literary agent Jenn Joel make suggestions and weigh in on all the other JV ideas, like mine.

"Well, Chris Cleave has a book coming out called *Little Bee*, which is going to be very successful," she'd say.

Or, "Billy Crystal's *700 Sundays* is now in hardcover. But let me check his tour schedule."

Someone would throw out an author's name and she'd respond, "Well, he lives in Michigan, but maybe he'd come in for it."

How did she know all this? I thought her insider knowledge was the coolest thing ever. She knew what was coming out and where the authors lived! Authors weren't fully formed people in my mind, just items on a wish list, inaccessible rock stars who typed in obscurity. I had had a pen-pal relationship as a kid with a middle grade author named Zibby Oneal that had culminated in her taking me for tea at the Plaza Hotel when she came to town. But insights like Jenn's? Amazing.

I piped up.

"What about Amanda Hesser's *Cooking for Mr. Latte*? Diane Johnson for *L'Affaire*? *Lucky Girls* by Nell Freudenberger? *The Namesake* by Jhumpa Lahiri?"

Every book I suggested, Jenn knew all about.

"She's not touring now."

"She's working on a new book."

"Maybe we wait for the paperback."

I stared at her across the table in awe.

Years later, Jenn would become my dad's agent. We would chat in the corner at some of my dad's various book-tour events and we sat together at his seventieth birthday celebration in Palm Beach. Every so often, I'd tell her about a book idea of mine, and she'd come right back with endless reasons why it wouldn't sell.

———

In the day-to-day moments of my stay-at-home mom life, I was constantly stressed. Playgroup in the park? On it! I'd rush around, making sure the diaper bag was perfect. Bath-time? Yes, but I had to race across town for a board meeting afterward.

Friends suggested gently that perhaps I had too much on my plate. The kids. All those boards. Perhaps I should step down from one of them?

Actually, I didn't have *too much* on my plate. No. My plate was just filled with all the wrong things. Instead of having grilled fish and a delicious ratatouille, my plate was overflowing with rotten spinach. I was busy, but I wasn't satisfied or happy. When I took something off my plate, it made things worse. I thought back to a time when I'd listed all my commitments on unused pages of my food diary. I'd climbed back on the Weight Watchers wagon post-twins and had gotten down to a size 4 again. I'd sit there puzzling over which commitments to cross off the list, always missing the right answer: I needed to add, not subtract.

Those days of twin toddlerhood were long. As soon as I woke up in the morning, I'd start counting down until I could go back to sleep again at night. Most days, I'd lose it. I'd snap. If one of the kids started having a tantrum, it raised my blood pressure so much it felt like my brain was swirling in a red sea. As the kid melted down, so would I. I would sneak into a closet or put my face in my pillow and scream. I couldn't manage it all. Everything was out of my control. The parenting books I read, like *1-2-3 Magic*, made it all sound so easy. Discipline was as simple as holding up your fingers and counting? When I counted to three, nothing happened!!

The kids didn't sleep well, which meant I never slept. I stopped smiling. It was all I could do not to cry in front of them.

When I was called for jury duty when the twins were three years old, I headed to Barnes & Noble on the Upper East Side and let them run around the children's area while I stocked up on help-your-kid-sleep books.

In the holding pen where I'd spend three days, I sank into a plastic chair, dropped my heavy tote at my feet, and pulled out my stack of ten sleep books. I wrote the key points in a notebook overflowing with strategies. I attacked the sleep issue like a final exam. I would solve this problem.

A middle-aged woman chuckled as she walked past me.

"It gets easier," she said, smiling.

———

The previous year, after months of not sleeping, of crying babies and feeding, pain and tears, and trying to stay on top of everything else in life, I'd collapsed.

I'd just given the kids a bath, kneeling on the tile floor beside the cool white lip of the tub while they splashed and played. But I couldn't stop crying. I tried to hide it from my twins, from everyone, but it wasn't working. When the kids got tired of playing in the tub, I picked up my son and wrapped him in a fluffy white towel, while Tenzin came in and picked up my daughter.

"Are you okay?" she asked.

I nodded, through tears.

I carried my happy toddler son down the hall, all cocooned and cuddled, and suddenly couldn't go another step. I sank onto the floor, putting him down next to me, and then, in a version of child's pose, I wailed. My face in the carpet fibers, my son on his back beside me, playing with his toes, the wet towel partially covering him, I sobbed. I couldn't function. I couldn't pick him up again. Tenzin called my mom and told her I needed help.

The next day, I was alone in the back of a black car on my way to the Mayflower Inn, a lovely hotel in Washington, Connecticut, with a restorative spa on a sprawling garden campus. Clearly, I needed more than a spa weekend, but this was the easiest thing for my loved ones to implement. My family insisted I take some time "off" to catch up on sleep. I just couldn't go on this run-down and depressed. I wasn't being a good mom.

The kids would be fine, my mom insisted.

I slept the whole car ride and headed straight to the spa.

Shoes weren't allowed inside the spa building, so I left my sneakers in the little cubby in the entry foyer and slid on the awaiting pair of slippers. Shuffling inside, my slippers sliding on the stone floor, I walked up to the front desk.

The attendant, a blonde, buxom woman with curly hair, a white polo shirt, and a name tag, looked up at me. I don't remember what I looked like, but I remember what she said.

"Oh, honey," she uttered. "You look like you really *need* to be here."

She came around the desk and walked with her arm around me into the main spa living room. I was greeted by soaring ceilings and giant windows that faced a lawn and forest. Pale-blue walls. White chenille chaise couches with cozy throws on each one were lined up like bowling pins facing the windows. A large chandelier hung over a table of magazines. Built-in tables and banquettes lined the walls. Everything about it radiated peace. Relaxation. Safety. Calm. The bright morning light bathed the Zen-like furniture in a warm, enveloping, golden tonic.

"Why don't you have a seat here and just relax? Rest a little bit."

The receptionist settled me into one of the chaises.

"Can I put some blankets on you?"

I nodded.

"Thank you so much."

My eyes filled with tears.

"I'm just so tired. I have twins. I haven't been sleeping."

There was more to it, but I wasn't going to share all the ins and outs.

"Well, you just rest while you're here. Let us take care of you, mama. I'll bring you some tea."

I closed my eyes that morning and didn't wake up again until dinnertime, the sky black outside, the day over. The receptionist had been replaced by a younger woman who smiled at me as I walked past the desk in search of my shoes. I slept in my room until the next morning.

When sunlight warmed the spa, I swam in the giant indoor pool, under a ceiling made of glass, and marveled at the brilliant blue sky overhead. I had to regroup. How had I let myself get so run-down?

Why did I feel so desperately alone? How could I do things better? I wrote, trying to sift through my emotions like piles of sand on a beach.

By the time I got home, after only forty-eight hours away, I was brimming with new energy, like a car pulling out from a gas station, full and dripping remnants of gasoline behind it. I was still depressed, but I had the inner resources to get help, find a new therapist, experiment with some new meds, and try to get back to baseline.

———

At night, after I had finally gotten the kids to bed, I would read to the hum of the sound machine, cracking open the spines of bestsellers, new and old. I flew through the Stieg Larsson Millennium series, starting with *The Girl with the Dragon Tattoo*. *Room* by Emma Donoghue. *Lit* by Mary Karr. *Open* by Andre Agassi. I read *It Sucked and Then I Cried: How I Had a Baby, a Breakdown, and a Much Needed Margarita* by Heather Armstrong, *The Summer We Read Gatsby* by Danielle Ganek, *I Feel Bad About My Neck* by Nora Ephron, *The Slippery Year* by Melanie Gideon, and *Black and Blue* by Anna Quindlen. I loved *A Million Little Pieces* by James Frey.

Actually, I was visiting my mom's apartment when the Oprah and James Frey interview aired.

"Zib, you have to watch this," my mom called from the other room.

"What?"

"That book we love! It's not real!"

I rushed into the family room in her apartment, the one where Howard was always watching sports.

I'd been obsessed with James Frey, recommending his book to anyone who would listen. When Oprah forced James to confess that what he'd written had been a fabrication, I grabbed my chest. I felt like I'd been cheated on. I held my hand over my heart in pain as I watched.

And yet, when *Bright Shiny Morning* and *My Friend Leonard* came out, I still snatched them off the shelf like a scorned lover allowed back into bed one last time. The passion of being wronged just upped the ante.

———

I attended author events frequently, arriving early to grab a good spot. The Barnes & Noble schedule from the *New York Times* clung to my fridge, barely staying affixed by Scotch tape. I usually went alone. My girlfriends enjoyed books, but not like I did.

Everyone was busy. Working. Dating. Volunteering.

Sometimes, it was just me and a couple of white-haired women in the audience. Occasionally, I would ask the authors questions about their writing processes, but usually I was too shy to speak up. The questions from the audience were typically bizarre. Random people would get up and talk for what felt like forever without even asking a question while the author sat mute, nodding, onstage.

Come on. I wanted to hear more! I wanted to hear what I didn't already know from the book jacket. I didn't want to listen to the author read from a book I already loved. I wasn't sure what exactly I was after, but it wasn't what I was getting. My favorite moments were when the author thanked her husband or her agent and I got to see who else was in their lives, like watching the proud wife cry when her husband won an Oscar. And yet, most weeks I'd try to attend another one, sitting in my hard plastic chair, hoping someone would ask a good-enough question to get the author to reveal something interesting.

There had to be a better way to get them to share.

E

2009–2014

Sixteen

Momzillas

"So, what do you do?"

I was standing by the carefully decorated, stocked bar at a private party at Juilliard. It was a friend's birthday and I'd thrown on a black dress, hastily applied eyeliner, and left the kids with Tenzin before bedtime, which I hated missing. There was already a crowd three-deep to get the signature cocktail of the night as music floated around us, the city lights peeking in through the floor-to-ceiling windows, a grand piano and other instruments waiting expectantly in the middle of the room for the big performance to come.

I didn't know how to answer.

I *never* knew how to answer.

If I told this acquaintance that I was a stay-at-home mom, I knew he'd either look bored and quickly search for someone more interesting to talk to or laud my decision and say, "It's the most important job there is!"

But really, was I "just" a stay-at-home? Was anyone?

For one thing, I was rarely at home. I was pushing the double stroller up and down Third Avenue, dodging elderly ladies and their ancient tiny dogs, on the way to music and gymnastics. I was walking the twins across Central Park all the way to the American Museum of Natural History once a week for hands-on science-and-nature class. I was running them to playgroups at various homes. Playdates. Preschool.

In between, there were the complicated processes of kid life management. Doctor appointments. Dentist. Eye doctor. Allergist. Was it time to sign up for camp? Flu shots? Birthday party gifts? Was I "enriching" them enough in their various activities? Were they falling behind? Did they need speech, occupational, or physical therapy? Did they seem gifted in any sports yet? Was there a sign-up I'd missed for the next fall?

And wait, let me stop all that and *be in the moment* and play on the floor until they get sick of me because *it all goes by too quickly*.

I was on multiple boards, planning events, raising money for charity. I was dealing with my home: making friends with the A/C guy and learning all about his wife's infertility problems as he changed the filters overhead, calling the plumber for that toilet, trying to find some sort of carpet-cleaning service. I wrote articles, read books like Justin Halpern's *Sh*t My Dad Says*, organized girls' dinners. I cooked for and with the kids, roasting chickens before preschool like Stacey and Connie had for me because my kids were always up early. I experimented with the various dishes I could make using olive oil, garlic, and ginger. Ordered FreshDirect. I was going to Weight Watchers meetings, school alumni events, social events, bookstore readings, and kids' birthday parties.

Did this hedge fund guy standing in front of me in a suit and Hermès tie care about any of that? How could I sum up my entire life in one brief answer?

"I'm a stay-at-home mom right now."

"Ah."

"How about you?" I asked.

"I work at a hedge fund."

"Ah."

I felt utterly pathetic.

I found a home video of the twins as toddlers recently. I could see myself in the background, racing like a maniac, packing for an upcoming trip, brow furrowed. Slim, with short, very dark brown hair and wearing a fitted pair of pants and a V-neck sweater, I was grabbing things and putting them into big boxy black duffels, moving back and forth, back and forth across the room.

The kids were smiling, laughing, preening for the camera. I wasn't paying any attention to them. I could literally see myself missing the moment, locked in my own head, crossing things off the endless to-do list.

I thought about that image of myself—frowning, busy, distracted, caught up in taking care of what was next instead of what was right there. I wanted to jump back in time and reorient myself toward the scene I was really in. What mattered.

———

My brother and I were having lunch outside at a restaurant in Tribeca on a crisp afternoon. I kept pulling my suede jacket tighter around me, readjusting the scarf wrapped around my neck. He was telling me about newlywed life and how he and his new wife, Ellen, were constantly making each other laugh.

"That's so great, Teds!"

"Yeah, things are good. It's nice."

I paused and thought for a second.

"I actually can't remember the last time I laughed."

"What do you mean?"

"I mean, I don't laugh. I never laugh anymore. I just don't."

His face grew sympathetic as he gently said, "Aw, Zib. That's terrible."

I hadn't even realized it until I told him. I knew I wasn't happy. I was seeing a new therapist, a cognitive behavior specialist who had me making charts, detailing things like why I flew off the handle if someone gave one of the kids a single Cheerio when it wasn't exactly the right time for them to eat.

When my twins went to day camp that summer, I would drive the blurry Route 114 to a spin class in Sag Harbor and cry all the way there, while on the bike, and all the way home.

———

But come on. How could I be sad when I was so lucky? How could I be depressed when I had beautiful twins, a home in the Hamptons, and such a life of privilege? *Shouldn't I just shut up and be grateful?*

Unfortunately, depression doesn't work that way. It's a heavy cloak that sits on your shoulders like the protective gear required for an X-ray machine. It doesn't choose its victims based on logic. It's an equal opportunity destroyer of souls.

I was also feeling guilty for *being* depressed, as if the neurochemical cocktail wasn't destructive enough.

I would beat myself up relentlessly, willing myself to just snap out of it. How could I be sad? What was wrong with me? I'd been battling depression and anxiety my whole life. I didn't stay in bed or pull the shades. I mostly just cried and waited for the anvil on my chest to lift. It struck often. I took solace in other people's ability to push through challenge, as in *Portrait of an Addict as a Young Man* by Bill Clegg, or Andrew Solomon's *The Noonday Demon.*

Now, as a middle-aged mom, I've learned to sniff out its impending arrival and to watch it descend. It no longer envelops me. I can be an impartial observer, even as it renders me incapacitated at times.

It always does lift, a fluttering bird that sometimes sweeps up close before banking upward and pitching away. Now I've gotten so good at managing it with medication and tools honed in therapy and years of practice that I can hide it, flipping a switch. I can "turn on" a happy version of myself, despite what I'm feeling. Most of the time.

And now, when I feel the depression, sometimes I write about it on Instagram or Medium, getting instantaneous connection, community, and support. The bird flies away after a quick flutter in my direction.

Seventeen

Disrupted

D o you have time to chat?"

I was standing in the hallway of the neighborhood temple, waiting for my twins to finish class.

"Definitely, yes."

It was a friend of Stacey's boyfriend, Bryan, named Matt Evans. He wanted to discuss a start-up he was launching with another HBS grad, a daily-deal site like Groupon, but for moms, called Gaggle of Chicks. During naptime, I ran over to a coffee shop on the Upper East Side that charges five-star-restaurant prices for diner food.

A year younger than me, with a boyish charm, Matt pitched me the business.

"We'll offer limited-time-only deals for things like kids' cooking classes and moms can buy them before they expire," he said. "I was hoping you could tell me what you think of this, as a mom, and if you have any places that are amazing and that we should reach out to."

"Wait, wait, wait," I said. "Back up. Tell me more about the business model. And what's your team like? Do you have investors?"

I didn't want to be a mom resource. I wanted to build his business.

By the end of our meeting—the thick diner coffee mugs filled with bland, watery coffee making rings on the Formica table between us—I'd made up my mind.

"I want to get involved," I said. "This sounds amazing. Can I help?"

"Let me check with my partner," Matt said. "We weren't expecting this, but it could be great. Can I get back to you after we speak?"

"Of course!"

I walked out of the coffee shop with Matt, waved goodbye, and headed back to the kids with a spring in my step. It wouldn't be a job, exactly. It could be a fun, part-time thing. I could still be a stay-at-home mom. But I wanted to do it.

That night, I had just finished giving the kids a bath when Matt called. I left them with Tenzin and rushed downstairs into my carpeted blue-and-white bedroom with the built-in white shelves lined with books. I closed the door behind me.

"Okay, I'm here!"

"Hey, great. So, yeah, we'd love to have you on board. As much or as little as you want to do is great. Just tell us what you want to do."

I hung up and literally started jumping up and down alone in my bedroom. I kept saying, "I have a job! I have a job! I have a job!"

I was going to be the GaggleMama blogger and help with strategy and sales.

Relief mixed with excitement as my dimples got a workout.

The next morning, I started. I came up with a list of companies and contacts to target. I outlined marketing strategies to spread the word to moms. Their logo and branding were already done, but I gave suggestions for how to improve the website. I launched the GaggleMama blog and started writing daily. I recruited talent and got a girlfriend to come on board to help with sales. The company started growing, quickly. There were two other competitors doing the exact same thing. How could we differentiate ourselves?

Gaggle grew over the next few months and got an office in Brooklyn. They hired two more sales team members. I was in charge of hiring the lead content contributor who would be writing everything on the site to make it more like *New York* magazine.

Whenever I took my kids to a class, I'd give my business card to the organizer and ask if they'd be interested in doing a group deal with Gaggle. My everyday life took on a new purpose. I wasn't aimlessly shaking toy tambourines at Little Maestros; I was negotiating a deal with them afterward.

The first team meeting was scheduled in Gaggle's new Brooklyn headquarters, a tiny section of a shared workspace in an industrial building.

My separation anxiety swirled over me like the tornado in *The Wizard of Oz*, that same wicked-witch music playing in my head on repeat. I was terrified to go to Brooklyn and leave the kids in Manhattan. What if something happened and I couldn't get back to them in time? What if there was another terrorist attack and Manhattan's border closed? What if something happened to all the bridges and tunnels? What if a kid got hurt and I couldn't be with them in the hospital? What if a bookcase fell on them and they had only a few minutes left to live and I was stuck in traffic trying to get back to see them and didn't make it in time?

What if?

Anxiety had come and gone for me as regularly as the seasons, but I was always surprised how much it changed the landscape. Although I'd found ways to cope through therapy and medication, anxiety always shaped how I saw the world. When I first found out that anxiety was even a thing, I was shocked. Didn't everyone worry like I did?

I asked a coworker to head to the meeting with me. As I drove across the Brooklyn Bridge to our Gaggle meeting, I talked back to my anxiety. I could go to one meeting. Everyone else commuted to and from Brooklyn all the time without anything happening. I could, too. I would be fine. The kids would be fine.

Even though I felt guilty every single second, I got back home in one piece.

But the fear I felt crossing the Brooklyn Bridge was oppressive.

At nights, I kept reading. *Seriously . . . I'm Kidding* by Ellen DeGeneres, *Bossypants* by Tina Fey, *The Chocolate Money* by Ashley Prentice Norton, *On Chesil Beach* by Ian McEwan, *Liar's Poker* by Michael Lewis, *Too Big to Fail* by Andrew Ross Sorkin, *The Year of Magical Thinking* by Joan Didion, *10% Happier* by Dan Harris, *The Happiness Project* by Gretchen Rubin, and *Poser: My Life in Twenty-Three Yoga Poses* by Claire Dederer.

I worked for Gaggle for almost a year, until it was acquired by a competitor. But during that year, I remembered how to think, how to be creative, how to write, how to use Facebook, and how to take my everyday life and turn it into something that helps build a business.

Eighteen

A Very Young Dancer

It was the ballet spot for the uptown set. I sat crisscross-applesauce on the cold linoleum floor in a studio at Ballet Academy East. The spartan decor, clanky lockers in the drab dressing rooms, and faded carpets seemed frozen in time from when I went as a little girl. My daughter twirled the tassels of her new ballet slippers as she sat in my lap in her pink leotard and tights. I waited for the class to begin, not recognizing any other mothers or daughters, but smiling politely at the others in the circle. I lost hope of any pre-class adult conversation. The pianist started playing on the grand piano in the corner of the room as the teacher twirled around.

Ten minutes later, the glass-front door to the classroom swung open and a gorgeous, blonde, smiling creature burst in, sat down next to me, and plunked her leotard-clad daughter down in front of her. She didn't seem stressed, her sense of humor coming through as she took off her scarf and bright-yellow jacket, nudged me, smiling, and said, "Fourth child."

"I'm always late," she added.

"I'm always early," I replied.

We spent the rest of the class quietly chitchatting despite the teacher's disapproving stares. Afterward, in her southern drawl, she said, "Okay, honey, I'll see you next week! I'm Paige, by the way."

I couldn't wait. Her eyes twinkled as she sauntered off, making parenting look like a fun game instead of a long slog.

The following September, my twins started preschool. I'd gotten the time wrong for their orientation and had sprinted from Second Avenue to Madison in my navy A-line shirt dress and heels, pushing the double stroller at superspeed so we wouldn't be late. I can still feel the sweat dripping down the inside of that dress as I met their first teachers, wondering if everyone could see it.

The first day of class, on time and prepared, I sat in a tiny wooden chair as the twins got settled in their new classroom. And then, in she walked. My friend from ballet. Paige Hardy.

I stood up before she saw me and then caught her eye. "Honey! We're in class together!" We hugged hello. "Oh, aren't *we* going to have fun. Okay, better go find my husband, Tripp. He's wandering around the building somewhere with my other daughter. Bye!"

Paige quickly became the slightly older mom who showed me the ropes, reassuring me that after-school classes didn't even matter and that, in fact, she didn't sign up for any of them. She showed me where the best seat was at preschool graduation. She reminded me constantly not to stress about kindergarten admissions.

All the moms in the preschool class were fantastic and we quickly formed what we later called "The Group Six Breakfast Club." Every month we'd go to one of our apartments after drop-off, sit around kitchen tables or in decorated living rooms and chat about our kids, our husbands, our lives. We laughed. We commiserated. We got and gave advice. We cried. When we were on duty, we helped each other do drop-offs and pickups, arranged playdates together, bathed each other's kids during sleepovers, and tucked them in like they were our own.

We were all pretty different individually—a Korean American banker, an internist from Boston, a Venezuelan consultant, several lawyers, many of us at home for the first time—but we jelled as a group. Ladies' drinks or rotating breakfasts at our homes, we were always in touch.

Paige quickly became our bandleader. Her hilarious stories about her army of five children had all of us in hysterics. We told each other things we wouldn't usually dream of sharing—mom confessions, fears. One mom told us how she'd accidentally used spray deodorant on her kids, thinking it was sunscreen. Another admitted how she'd shown up to a birthday party an entire day late. Paige shared intimate physical facts about her kids that we were kind of horrified to hear. But we quickly became a team. Partners-in-arms. In the trenches together as only fellow parents can be.

While many of our Breakfast Club moms left our preschool after two years, Paige and I both had kids with summer birthdays, so we stayed a third year with a new crop of parents.

———

She texted me one morning. Could I bring home her daughter after school? Of course. She texted later that day as I watched my kids and her daughter build a fort in my living room.

Okay, don't say anything to anyone, but I'm getting some tests done. I'm at the hospital. Can you keep her a bit longer?

Of course.

I found out later that she'd been on the street on the way to Whole Foods and had so much trouble breathing that she called her husband, who insisted she see a doctor.

"But what about the milk?" she had asked.

I kept her daughter as Paige stayed overnight in the hospital.

My daughter woke me.

"I think something's wrong . . ." she said, nudging me.

I zoomed up out of bed just in time to find Paige's daughter vomiting on the hallway carpet just outside my door.

Later, Paige would regale our group and say, "When I found out, I was like, 'Dear Lord, she just ruined a million-dollar carpet.'"

The next few days brought more tests. I tried to stay out of it, but how could I?

She called me from the hospital.

"I'm going to miss all the school curriculum nights!" she said. "I keep telling the doctors I can't stay here any longer!"

"I'll take notes," I said. "Don't even worry. You're lucky you don't have to go!"

Our mutual friend texted me the news. Paige was diagnosed with stage 4 ovarian cancer. No family history. No reason. How could it be that this Kentucky native who had burst on the New York social scene, making it seem like an afternoon at the derby, was sick? I can still see her driving her giant white SUV, pulling up to preschool and shooing her four-year-old out of the car and up the steps, smiling ear to ear from the front seat with a "better late than never" attitude.

Paige was also passionately in love with her husband. She always said things like, "Isn't my husband just the hottest thing?" Once at a Breakfast Club cocktail hour, she told a group of us, "It was such a nice night out last night that I called Tripp around 5 p.m. and said, 'Honey, drop everything, we're going for drinks at the Surrey.'"

I said, "Wait, what'd you do with all your kids?"

She laughed.

"I called my sitter and she just put them to bed! I had to have a date with my gorgeous husband."

As a mother drenched in anxiety, I couldn't believe her carefree attitude. Skip bedtime at the last second? Was that even an option? Paige referred to her own family as the Hardy Party. She even had stickers made up with the name.

Before I knew it, I was dropping off taco-night kits for her kids while she battled it out at Memorial Sloan Kettering, hosting her daughter frequently for playdates, communicating with all the many other friends she had.

In the midst of treatment, she'd tell us all stories. She would flirt with her doctors, bat her eyelashes with her southern charm, and say, "Honey, I've got five children. I'm not going anywhere."

She decided that Tuesdays, chemo days, would be leopard Tuesdays. Every Tuesday morning, Paige would text me and a few other close friends pictures of her from the chemo room with her assorted leopard wear, still looking like a fashion model, her bright-red lipstick on. All around the city, from Doubles to Central Park playgrounds, women would be wearing leopard print for her.

Paige started losing her hair. She brought her five kids in the bathroom with her and asked them to shave it all off. She wore a wig with a leopard-print hat on. All the while, our Group Six Breakfast Club continued to meet. She'd tell us all the details of her treatment, how she was managing the kids, how amazing Tripp was being. Then she'd quickly turn it over to us, just as interested in our ordeals applying to schools or spats with our own husbands.

For a while, she seemed completely in charge of the cancer. I think she scared that ovarian cancer into remission. Her deep faith in God, her constant imploring of everyone to pray for her, the strength she exhibited, it all combined with luck and medicine to smash it.

She beat it!

Her hair started growing back in. She was out and about again, on the society scene, attending five school curriculum nights in two weeks, planning fun outings, sending thoughtful thank-you gifts from her "Hardy Party" gift closet. It wasn't unusual for me to open a gift bag she gave me as a thank-you for hosting her for dinner and find a Halloween Jell-O mold (in April), a notepad with a clever saying, a cow-shaped pancake maker, and a *Frozen* Elsa microphone.

One morning, Paige filled the basement of St. James' Church, giving a speech to one hundred women, telling us all her story again, inspiring those she hadn't met, making us laugh and cry. We went back to our Breakfast Club events, lunches with our crew, lingering on couches with coffee, sitting around our friend Carrie's kitchen table, laughing, crying, getting through motherhood, getting through life. That spirit, that laughter, always fills my soul on Tuesday mornings.

Nineteen

THE TIPPING POINT

I'd always wanted three or more kids. Growing up, it had just been Teddy and me. When my parents got divorced, instead of feeling like a family of four, it often felt like a family of two, moving between homes like a raft bobbing on the surface of a rippling pool. When my brother grew up and claimed his rightful independence, it felt like my family had become a series of lunches and dinners, combinations and permutations, more than a rousing full unit.

Splintered. It was a primal, deep need, to have enough kids that they would always be a crew unto themselves.

I kept telling myself that I already had two kids, a boy and a girl, that I was so lucky. Why did I want another child so badly? Why wasn't I satisfied?

A third child didn't seem to be in the cards. After I'd given up and donated all my old baby supplies, my boobs started hurting. They ached so badly that I called my doctor to see what I could do about it. She told me to take some Saint-John's-wort and that it was probably premenstrual. Or perimenopausal.

Nope. Turns out it was my daughter.

In the hospital on the night she arrived, I was so excited to get to know her that I couldn't sleep. Forget the plastic bassinet on top of the wooden cart beside me. I wasn't letting go.

With the lights dim and the beeps and blips of hospital life threatening to drown out our fairy-tale moment, I grabbed my phone and played Van Morrison, singing to my little one as she smiled up at me. She wasn't supposed to be able to smile or have such meaningful eye contact on day one. But she did.

We swayed to the music in my hospital bed as I cooed the lyrics. *We were born before the wind . . .*

I played song after song in that dark room, just the two of us.

———

My daughter was a month old. I sat on the bathroom stool, hooked up to the yellow milk-extraction contraption. A book was propped up against the machine so I could read while I pumped: *Z: A Novel of Zelda Fitzgerald* by Therese Anne Fowler.

I could hear my twins, now age six, in my office just through the doorway.

"What's 'add to cart'?"

Uh-oh.

"What are you guys up to out there?" I yelled.

"Nothing!"

They snickered.

"Guys? What are you up to?"

"Nothing!"

They both came running in a minute later. My son had a mischievous glint in his eye, a wide smile showing his dimples.

After the milk was sealed away in labeled plastic baggies and the eight thousand pieces of the pump were washed and set on paper towels to dry, I went back into my office. Everything seemed okay.

Three days later, I was opening up that day's delivery of Amazon boxes. I tore through the brown tape and found a giant telescope.

"What the—?"

My son ran over.

"My telescope! It came!"

"What?"

"I ordered it on Amazon!"

Years later, my fourth child, another boy, would pull a similar trick on my phone, ordering four giant boxes packed with *Paw Patrol* toys, which arrived at our front door, much to his glee. I ended up getting interviewed by the *Wall Street Journal* and appearing on *Good Morning America* to describe what happened.

He was also a complete gift from God. I was still reeling from my daughter's arrival, delighting in knowing what it was like to have just one baby at a time and not being a first-time mom.

When I went for my physical, my doctor, a curly-haired, jovial man, suggested I get a bone density scan. I'd had issues with osteopenia years earlier; when I was so restrictive in my eating, my bones had literally started deteriorating.

He typed in a request for some standard blood tests and, before adding the bone density scan to the list, looked up and said, "Any chance you might be pregnant?"

"Ha!"

I laughed.

"My daughter is only eight months old."

"I just have to ask," he said.

I paused as he moved on.

Actually, I hadn't had my period lately. But I was nursing and that made everything wonky.

Nah. Couldn't be.

"Well, I guess it's possible . . ."

He looked up again.

"I'll just add a pregnancy test to the mix. You never know. And let's hold off on getting the scan for now."

A few days later when he called me with the other results, I said, "So that pregnancy test was negative, too, right?"

I could hear his keys clicking.

"Hmm. Looks like the lab didn't run that test after all. Maybe just pick up a home pregnancy test, so we can dot all our i's and cross all our t's."

"Okay," I said.

A few days later, when the big kids were at school and my third was napping, I ran across the street and picked up a home pregnancy kit, then popped into my bathroom and quickly peed on the stick. I just wanted to get it over with and let the doctor know.

I put the test on the toilet lid to work its magic while I fired off a few emails at my desk. I walked back in a few minutes later to throw it in the trash can.

Pregnant.

I gasped, ran out of the bathroom, and slammed the door shut, leaving the stick in there.

No. I couldn't be having another baby. I *had* a baby!

I stood there, frozen, panting, a hand on my heart.

I tiptoed back to the toilet and peered at the stick again.

Still pregnant.

A couple of minutes later, after leaving the baby with Tenzin, I burst into my doctor's office with the stick in my hand, shaking.

"Look!" I said to the receptionist.

"Come right on in."

The rapid test at the doctor's replicated my findings.

Sitting in the exam room, I put my head in my hands. How on earth was I going to manage four kids? The moms I knew who had four kids were all so laid-back. Relaxed! How could I possibly, as a type-A mom, pull this off? It was impossible. And how could I give my older kids enough attention? And my new baby!

My OB came in, a fellow mom of twins who was just a smidge older and much wiser than me.

"I know this was unexpected," she said. "There are options we can discuss."

"No, I don't need options," I said. "I just . . . I don't know how I'll be able to do this . . . I'm shocked."

I descended into books, losing myself in others' stories as I sorted out my own unexpected ending. *This Is Where I Leave You* by Jonathan Tropper and *The Goldfinch* by Donna Tartt did the trick.

With a fourth on the way, I was sure I'd never have time to see friends again. I decided to throw a party called: "#4 and no more." I even made personalized napkins. Paige and the Breakfast Club were there, smiling in all the party photos.

I never got that bone density scan.

N

2014–2015

Twenty

OPEN

My son and I burst through the front door of the East Hampton Indoor Tennis club. It was a bitter-cold, snowy December morning and I was late and exhausted, two weeks postpartum with my little guy. My younger daughter had cried and screamed as I'd left the house, sobbing with her tiny palm on the frosted window as I drove off. And my older son really didn't want to be here.

"Mom, I hate tennis," he'd said that morning.

"I know, sweetie," I'd responded, grabbing his racket from the top shelf of the mudroom and throwing his tennis shoes in my tote bag as he stood there in his bright-orange Denver Broncos sweatpants and matching jersey. "But playing tennis is really good for you. It's great exercise, and it's fun! You can lie around the house the rest of the day, but now you just have to play tennis for thirty minutes. Okay? That's it. Come on, let's go."

"But, Mom," he said, "you're not listening to me. I want to play football."

"I'm listening," I said. "But it's too cold out to play football, so today you're playing indoor tennis. You'll have a great time once you're on the court with Fabio. Now let's go! We're going to be late."

I just wanted my son to get some exercise. I wanted some semblance of structure in the kids' Christmas break from school. Indoor tennis on a Saturday morning in December in East Hampton seemed like the best solution.

I'd been up since 5:00 a.m. with the baby. We had nothing planned for two weeks, the days stretching ahead of me like an empty highway in a hurricane. My iCal was empty except for tennis. I knew I needed to "take it easy" after my C-section, but the lack of structure filled me with anxiety.

My son had complained the whole drive there.

"Can't I just play an hour of football instead?"

"Honey, there's snow everywhere. There's no place to go play football. You can keep playing football in the house, but it's good for you to get out and run around. And you love Fabio!"

Fabio was the charming Brazilian tennis pro who had delighted my son by playing a game called Fireball, in which he swatted an entire basket of balls at him as he ran around the exterior of the court, trying to avoid getting hit. My son loved it. It wasn't exactly tennis, but whatever. It was something to do. I'd read *Open* by Andre Agassi recently and couldn't get enough tennis myself.

I'd caught a glimpse of my face in the rearview mirror. My hair was pulled back into a messy bun. No makeup, just black circles under my bloodshot eyes. My face was swollen and puffy, my body a wreck. I'd barely gotten dressed; I'd just thrown on the unfashionable faded black yoga pants I'd had for about six years with an oversize gray fleece that had expanded to fit me at nine months pregnant. Plus white tennis shoes.

I'd pulled the giant SUV into the gravel parking lot. My son was leisurely tying his shoes.

"The lesson started two minutes ago. Let's GO!"

Then we burst in.

I scanned the pro shop quickly for Fabio.

"Hey, buddy! I'm going to be teaching your lesson today!"

What? I jerked my head around to look toward the unfamiliar voice. Who was this guy? Young. Tan. Curly brown hair. Athletic build. Kind brown eyes. Fabulous smile. Definitely not Fabio.

"Hi. What do you mean?" I asked. "Where's Fabio?"

"He had to go out of town, so I'm covering his lessons. I'm Kyle," he said, giving a little wave.

No one had told me there would be a substitute. I would've rescheduled. My son was going to lose it. I couldn't even look at him.

"I'm Zibby," I responded.

"No way! I have a friend named Sibby!"

"Oh, okay."

I was too tired to care. I turned to face my son's wrath.

"I'm not playing," he said, arms crossed.

"Honey, just go out. It'll be fun!"

"Come on, buddy!" Kyle said. "You got this!"

Kyle opened the door to the bubble. My son reluctantly followed him, glaring at me.

I collapsed into the closest chair. Finally, I could have thirty minutes "off." To just sit. Read the newspapers. Breathe. I was beyond excited. I pulled the papers out of my bag and started reading, occasionally looking through the giant glass window to check in on the lesson.

A few minutes later, the woman at the reception desk suddenly called out to me. "Excuse me? I think Kyle is trying to get your attention."

"Me?"

She pointed to the court.

Kyle was at the net, motioning for me to join them. *What the . . . ?* I put down the papers with a beleaguered sigh and headed down the long corridor past the other indoor courts to the sound of thwacking balls. I pulled open the heavy plastic cloak to walk onto their court.

"Hey!" Kyle said, all smiles as I approached the net. "So, listen. Your son really doesn't like tennis."

I paused. We just looked at each other for a moment.

"I know that," I responded slowly.

"He's really into football!"

"Yes. I know that, too."

"Okay, well, I don't think you should be wasting your money by giving him a lesson if he really doesn't want to play."

I think I may have laughed out loud. It was all too much. The cold. The baby. The C-section. The kids. The tennis. I couldn't accomplish a single thing. And now this young guy with his mop of thick brown hair and inexplicably tan skin was standing there, messing up my plan. Yes, I knew it sounded odd that I was "forcing" my son to play tennis. But what did Kyle know about parenting?

"Well, I do," I finally said.

"Well, he won't be taking lessons with me."

My jaw dropped. Even my son gasped a little. Seriously, this guy wasn't going to teach my son?

"I just prepaid for his lessons," I replied.

"Well, maybe you can get your money back."

We just stared at each other.

I had to give Kyle some credit. He had his standards, respect for his craft. That was refreshing. But really, who *was* he? I found out later that he'd been a tennis coach for some players on the WTA Tour, a tennis tournament director, and head of the tennis program at a well-known academy. He was filling in for Fabio, but he had his limits.

He turned to my son.

"See you later, buddy! And if you decide you want to play Fireball, Fabio will be back next week. That just isn't how I teach."

He gave my son a high five and wheeled his cart of balls off the court, leaving the two of us at the net, shocked.

"I told you, Mom," my son said as we regrouped. "I really don't like tennis."

As it turned out, I couldn't get my money back for the lesson. So, given my own love of tennis, I asked for a credit, which I ended up redeeming myself for weekly lessons with Kyle come spring. If he was really that great, I wanted to see what all the fuss was about.

———

Tennis had been a part of my childhood, tied up with so many memories. I can still smell the inside of my family's Chevrolet Caprice classic station wagon. I can feel the tan leather bench seats, the sand-colored carpet on the floor under my toes, my Tretorns and white socks with little pom-poms tossed to the side. Billy Joel belted out of the tinny speakers, singing about uptown girls and downtown boys, as our wagon glided down Route 27 in the Hamptons.

The trunk, which we called "the way back," somehow converted into a third row that faced backward, looking out the narrow rear window. We were allowed to change it to a seat only on special occasions. I can't remember which friend of mine vomited in our trunk. The front row was another bench seat with an armrest in the middle, which we called "the special seat." Teddy and I used to fight over who got to sit there. He usually won. Seat belts? Never. We were all incredulous when wearing seat belts became a law and we had to buckle up.

The ashtray was always full. My mother would drive us to tennis with one hand on the wheel, the other hand bringing her Vantage premium cigarettes back and forth to her red lips, her nails lacquered in bloodred each week, thanks to her standing appointment with Bella.

Ash. Inhale. Exhale.

Now Billy Joel was an innocent man. My mom tapped her fingers on the wheel.

Ash. Inhale. Exhale.

I was usually in the middle row, staring out the window. There was no traffic in the Hamptons then. "The Hamptons" weren't even a thing. We called it "the country." Our house, built in 1979, was surrounded by potato fields. I remember feeling jealous of my school friends, who all went to places like Fishers Island and Martha's Vineyard. No one I knew from the city went to the Hamptons. But we had our own community out there—our family friends, a tight-knit crew.

On Sunday nights, we would all convene for cookouts on Georgica Beach. Our boom box played tapes, quilts were spread out, with red paper plates rustling in the wind, and sand was scattered lightly over our hot dogs and burgers. Weekend days would find us at someone's home for a birthday party. More blankets on the ground, this time with slices of homemade cake, maybe some Kathleen's Cookies, before the company rebranded as the omnipresent "Tate's." Later, there would be cupcakes from Barefoot.

There were no bouncy castles except at festivals. We played capture the flag and musical chairs and ate pastel-colored dots off strips of white paper and left carrying personalized sand buckets. Our parents would ignore us, congregating on plastic lawn furniture. The women smoked, the dads stood around laughing. Occasionally, I would run over to my dad and grasp onto his leg, listening to the soothing baritone sounds of his conversation, words like "capital" and "net profit" and "merger" seeping out over the noise of the local musician playing his guitar. I loved hiding out in plain sight, listening, watching, just being near my dad. Then I'd run back to join the other kids. Sometimes I'd sit on my mom's lap while she stroked my hair, usually fashioned in a "pony on the side" with a color-coordinated ribbon.

On weekday afternoons, we played tennis. My mom drove the carpool, all of us dressed in our finest whites, tennis dresses with tennis bloomers underneath, crisp white shorts and polo shirts. We would turn off Route 27 into the East Hampton Indoor Tennis club, bumping down the long dirt-and-gravel driveway until we pulled into a parking lot filled with stones. A two-sided backboard was on the left as we drove in. As soon as my mom shifted the baton-like gearshift up into park, I'd usually hop out and hit against the backboard for a few minutes. I loved that no matter where I hit it, the ball would come right back to me with equal speed. My brother would run after me. Sometimes we chased one ball on the backboard, running and laughing.

We didn't go to any of the private country clubs in the Hamptons back then: the Maidstone, the Meadow Club.

Driving past them, my mother would whisper, "They don't take Jews."

I didn't understand what that meant or why, but I knew that anytime I drove by those formidable clubhouses, I would jut my chin out in protest and cross my arms protectively. I still have trouble going to the Maidstone as a guest.

No one had their own tennis court in the early 1980s. I can't remember a single family that had one, although by the time I reached high school, courts had popped up at every other house.

The wide gray stone slabs made a trail into the tennis clubhouse, if you could even call it that. There was a desk, a giant court schedule with pencil scribbles assigning courts and times, lessons and clinics. A few white iron tables with umbrellas and uncomfortable chairs rested on the patio in front with a view of the beautiful clay courts. When I stood up, the crisscross pattern of the chairs would be imprinted on my thighs. Copies of books like *Scruples* by Judith Krantz were left behind, dog-eared and worn.

The three hard courts where we had our clinic were down the hill and out of sight. To the right of the front desk and around the corner was the snack bar. A college student would peek out from behind a double-sided sliding partition, like in an old-fashioned taxi, to take our order and then help prepare it. Tuna salad sandwiches. Egg salad. FrozFruit bars. Frozen Snickers. If we hit a target in one of the drills during the clinic, we could go to the snack bar afterward and claim our reward: a can of Sunkist.

The few moms that gathered would sit by the snack bar and chat while we played. No one came down the hill to watch us. Sometimes the moms would show up in their own tennis skirts and tops and play some doubles after applying Fashion Tan SPF 2 to their tanned, toned arms and legs, their L.L.Bean tote bags left unattended on the tables. Prince racket covers, perhaps a Yonex, too, piled up in empty chairs.

Ping. Ping. Ping. Silence. Ping. Ping. Ping.

The sound of balls rhythmically bouncing back and forth over the net echoed across the many courts, with an occasional cry of "Sorry!"

Ping. Ping. Ping.

Every year on my birthday, when I'd enjoy dinner at the Palm on Main Street and a tennis court–shaped cake, maybe a quick trip to Penny Lane for some Pez, I'd wish for a new tennis racket. The years that I actually got one—because I definitely didn't get what I wished for most holidays—I'd fawn over it as if it were a diamond necklace, touching every part of it with my fingertips, carefully pulling out the information card from the gray plastic case (Prince Junior Pro) and writing my name and address. I can still remember the tangy, leathery smell of that case when I unzipped it on the court to play. I can hear the crack as the metal lid of a can of balls was sliced open and the scent of the balls exploded out of the plastic sleeve. Tennis was always such a sensory experience for me.

As I got older, I continued playing. I was captain of my JV high school team. As I previously recounted, Avery and I went on a teen tour trip called Tennis: Europe. I played intramural tennis at Yale occasionally and then in evening clinics after work when I lived in LA with Josh. I even played at business school whenever the weather held.

Tennis was a perfect way for me to relax, to stop the incessant thoughts in my brain, the debates, the logistics, the stresses, the oppressive perfectionism and anxiety. When I played tennis, I mostly thought about the strokes. How to make each shot better than the last. Bend your knees. Bring the racket back sooner. Keep your head down. Catch the racket on the upswing. Move your feet. Take small steps. It erased everything else.

As rewarding as motherhood was, it wasn't easy. Tennis? That was joy. That sense of accomplishment, power, and freedom. The satisfaction of an overhead slam. The sensation of pounding the ball over the net. The ping of a well-placed volley. That was a language I spoke fluently. One that would soon lead to a new kind of love.

Twenty-One

IT's HOT IN THE HAMPTONS

F ast-forward to summer. The Hamptons at their best. Farm stands on the side of the road selling overpriced strawberries. Sunflowers flowing out of the entrance to the local grocery store. Copies of the *East Hampton Star* on coffee tables, next to *Hamptons* magazines. Rosé all day. Corn salad and fresh tomatoes. Beautiful beaches. The stretch of traffic on Route 27 as far as the eye could see.

I'd had a horrendous morning with the kids. I hadn't slept. The twins wouldn't get ready for camp. The camp bus was waiting outside and they still hadn't put their shoes on. The little ones were screaming. I was overwhelmed, exhausted, and spent.

As I'd raised my voice again to yell, my older daughter had looked up at me and said, "Mama, I just want a hug."

After I watched the bus pull out of the driveway, I sat down on the front steps and cried, head in my hands. I couldn't do anything right. I'd misread her emotions. I hadn't coped correctly. Being late was a blinking neon sign advertising failure. It always made me feel inadequate, out of control. Time was the one thing I could control, usually. And I was late again for tennis.

When I got to the tennis club to take that lesson with Kyle, there he was, waiting for me at the front desk, smiling. I could feel a wave of energy wash over me like beams of sunlight, something twinkly and magical, a magnetic force of sorts. It wasn't that I was instantly attracted to him, although I did think he was adorable. It was some sort of deeper connection, the feeling that I'd already known him forever, that he was some sort of home.

"Hey!" he said. I wiped my eyes from crying in the car. "You ready?"

We started walking down the indoor court hallway side by side as I struggled to keep in my tears.

"I'm so sorry I'm late," I said.

"Don't worry about it!"

"It was just a really tough morning."

I didn't want to, but I started crying again.

"Oh no! Are you okay?"

Kyle stopped and put his arm around my shoulders like a concerned friend.

"Do you want to cancel the lesson?" he asked.

"No, no, it's okay."

I turned and looked at him. I couldn't believe he—a stranger!—was so sympathetic and understanding. Warm. Concerned. Connected. Something changed during that walk. Kyle would later tell me that he had experienced an unexpected physical sensation when he first touched me that felt magical, like he never wanted to let go, that it was his job to protect me. If it were a comic book drawing, there would be electric sparks flying as we both stopped to look at the impact of his innocent hand on my shoulder. A little bit of the universe had seeped in. We both tried to ignore it and kept walking.

But as we hit balls that day and in the days and weeks to follow, I found myself indescribably drawn to him. He made me laugh and seemed to resuscitate me in an elemental way just from spending time together.

Summer life with the kids moved on. Early morning swimming while the fog still bounced gently off the grass in the backyard. Brushing hair before the bus came for summer camp pickup.

"Where's that detangler spray?"

"Ow, MOM!"

Bottles, bottles, and more bottles for the baby. Washing bottles. Heating bottles. Burps that didn't seem to come fast enough. Pushing the toddler on the swings in town. Pool playdates in the afternoon. Books before naps. Body wash, shampoo, and conditioner in the bath. Singing: "Everybody do the body wash. Body wash!" Tucking in tired kids, the smell of oat milk–calendula lotion, the din of the sound machine lulling them to sleep. I often sat on the threshold of their rooms in the outline of the doorframe, reading a book like *All the Light We Cannot See* by Anthony Doerr or *The Boys in the Boat* by Daniel James Brown until their little bodies breathed in and out rhythmically, sound asleep.

Then, finally, the house was still. Toys put away. Clean bottles turned upside down on paper towels next to the sink. The dishwasher thrumming. All four kids safe and sound in bed.

I'd tiptoe down to the kitchen and poke around the cupboards. I never knew what I was trying to find in there, and I could never find it. Afterward, I'd sit on the light-blue tufted couch that was missing a couple of buttons, handed down to me from my stepmother, with a crinkly clear cellophane bag of chocolate-covered caramel candies. I'd pop the little chocolate orbs into my mouth by the handful, feeling my pulse quicken as the sugar surged into my system. In my faded white-and-black-striped pajama pants and long-sleeve shirt, I'd fold my legs on the couch, the quiet surrounding me like a long-lost friend, punctuated only by the crinkling cellophane. Then I'd open my laptop.

In the midst of the evening email catch-up on playdate scheduling, special camp announcements requiring bizarre things ("Rainbow tie-dye day tomorrow! Don't forget tie-dye socks!"), and class changes ("Gus Guitar class will be at Danielle's house Thursday!!"), I started texting with Kyle.

Twenty-Two

The Singles Game

Kyle, I quickly learned, had gone to culinary school. He'd almost become a chef instead of a tennis pro. But what he really wanted in life was to be in entertainment. I was intrigued.

After tennis one morning, I had to rush off to my daughter's art class in town. It was an overpriced but beautiful four-person arts and crafts workshop where we did things like paint leaves. If I'd been more creative and less tired, perhaps I could have come up with educational activities like this each week myself. But with four kids, I was more than happy to sit on the floor and glue seeds to construction paper for a few minutes with some mom friends.

I spent art class painting multicolored dots with my little one to create a forest, chatting with my three friends. I tickled my daughter's soft, juicy little thighs as she painted in my lap, musing about Kyle, replaying our conversations.

Later, in the middle of the night, I'd pat my baby's back to get him to return to sleep, shushing him to no avail, and find myself wondering what Kyle was doing, who he was dating, who he was out with that night.

As the tennis lessons continued, Kyle would tell me about his antics and adventures and I'd give him some advice. I didn't care. I just knew

I wanted to be closer to him. I started to count down between lessons and measured time between our interactions.

———

My best friend from high school, Gen, was visiting with her three kids. Tall, fit, with giant blue eyes, light-brown hair, gorgeous skin, and an amble as she walked, Gen was the one who would throw open her arms and hug any stranger on the street. A horse lover, Gen really should've been living in Montana and wearing a cowboy hat instead of doing kid pickups off the Philadelphia Main Line. She always seemed a little out of place, tumbling around in heels and nice clothes as a successful attorney.

It was summer houseguest chaos. Syrup bottles and napkins were strewn all over the kitchen as though I were operating a country diner. Random unclaimed flip-flops were scattered throughout the house. Wet towels draped over newly upholstered couches. Dripping bathing suits hung from door handles. My current book, *The Blessing of a Skinned Knee* by Wendy Mogel, sat on the counter. A dozen people in my house were making it a mess, and order was my sanity.

Gen and I sat side by side on stools at my kitchen island, our oversize white mugs steaming with freshly Keurig-ed coffee, as the kids played in the yard. I could see Tenzin out there watching over the jungle gym hijinks. The baby was still sleeping. We had a minute.

"So, I've started to question everything about life," I said.

"Well, that's a lot before breakfast."

"I'm serious. Are *you* truly happy?"

"Is anyone?"

I sighed.

"You're in the weeds, Zwibble," Gen said. "It's going to get easier."

My daughter came toddling in.

"Mama?"

"To be continued," I said. "I need to tell you about this guy . . ."

Later that day, Gen was lounging on a chaise by the pool with her eyes closed, not really watching my big kids as she'd promised, as her three older kids frolicked on oversize inflatable swans in the pool.

I plunked down next to her.

"Kinda enjoying heaven out here right now," she said.

"Mom! Come in the pool!" my son called.

"Two minutes, sweetie. I'm trying to talk to Aunt Gen."

"Moooom!"

Gen laughed. "We'll try again later."

That night, Gen and I left the kids all watching a movie together for a quick sunset drink, the only time I'd ever been to the celebrity-filled Montauk hot spot called the Surf Lodge. We chatted as the sun dove down into the rippling water, strategizing about life, love, and lessons, a copy of *The Five Love Languages* by Gary Chapman dog-eared between us. I confessed to Gen that I couldn't stop thinking about Kyle. I decided to take her to my tennis lesson the next day.

Twenty-Three

THE BRIDGES OF MADISON COUNTY

Gen and I walked down the corridor to the court. I'd persuaded her to play. Clay caked our shoes, balls pinged around us, and abandoned grocery carts filled with pressurized kids' balls with green dots had been left in the makeshift hallway.

"Hey, rock star!" Kyle belted out as I pulled aside the heavy plastic curtain and entered the bubble.

"Hi," I said. "I brought my friend Gen."

"Hi, friend Gen," he said. "You guys ready to play?"

"Oh yeah!" Gen said. "I've heard a lot about you."

Oh my God. I wanted to die. I felt like a teenager.

"Oh yeah?" he responded, smiling at me.

We warmed up with mini-tennis as he and Gen got to know each other. Where are you from? How old are your kids? I noticed Kyle wincing a few times. Months later I found out he'd torn a ligament in his arm the evening before but had still come out to play because he didn't want to miss our lesson.

When it was time to pick up the first bucket of balls, Kyle came over and handed me a wire ball basket, keeping one for himself.

"Everything okay?" he asked, starting to pick up balls. "You seem a little off."

"I'm fine," I said quietly, eyes averted. "You?"

I was suddenly beyond shy. I'd admitted my feelings out loud to Gen. She was watching. I was a bit embarrassed.

"Okay, you two," Gen yelled. "Stop all the chatting. Let's hit."

———

As I sat at our golf club the following week, the perfectly groomed rolling hills undulating in front of me, watching my kids take golf lessons on the driving range, I started thinking about Kyle but wanted to take my mind off him.

At the clubhouse, I decided to reread an essay I'd written for *Redbook* about losing Stacey. Stacey's mother, Martha, had recently given me Stacey's old red boa, the one that used to hang from the back of her bedroom door, ready for a night out. I'd written about how my own daughter had then used it to play dress-up, twirling in circles as I'd sat on the stairs watching her, crying, teaching her what "happy sad" meant. I wanted Stacey's loss to help me through, to help me figure out what to do, to tell me if I should follow my heart. I texted Kyle a link to the essay.

I don't know where you're waking up this morning—or with who—but thought you might like this article I wrote.

It turns out, he had woken up with someone. He'd saved my essay until that night when he was home, and he read it lying on his back, tears streaming down the sides of his face as he thought about his own relationship with his lifelong best friend, Don.

You're my favorite writer, he wrote. I'm crying.

The essay took our relationship one step deeper. (Thank you, Stace.)

I turned back to classic romances like Nicholas Sparks's *The Notebook* and *The Bridges of Madison County* by Robert James Waller. I needed to believe in romance. Love. My life was filled with Desitin diaper cream, not destiny.

My home life had so many positives: my beautiful children; my blessed, fortunate existence. And yet.

I'd recently developed a trick for not crying while reading out loud to the kids. Instead of reading the "treehouse down a sunny dirt road," I would read the words aloud, but in my head, I would simultaneously count the number of letters in each word. Nine. Four. One. Five. Four. Four. It would distract me enough to get to the next paragraph. I wouldn't have to hear one of them say, "Don't cry, Mama," or even watch them laugh that nervous laugh kids give when they don't understand what's going on.

The summer would end in a few days. I wouldn't see Kyle anymore; he was staying in East Hampton for his position at the club and I was going back for the kids' school and my life. I listened to songs like "Hold My Hand" by Jess Glynne, "Dancing on My Own" by Robyn, "The Fix" by Nelly, and "Praying" by Kesha. I tore through Jojo Moyes's *Me Before You.*

I realized I'd found my magical soul mate, as if God had plopped the perfect man right into my lap or, as my mother would later say, "He appeared like manna from heaven!" But should I really act on it? Did he feel the same way? He couldn't possibly. I was a mess. *What now?*

———

A mom friend from the kids' school invited me to join a group of women for an afternoon out on a boat to celebrate her fortieth birthday. I couldn't say no. When I boarded the boat in Sag Harbor, I found a full bar, an elaborate spread of food and sweets, a DJ, personalized towels, and a stack of paddleboards. I hadn't seen anything that wild and fun for someone turning forty. I still had a year to go myself.

The boat pulled away from the shore, music blasting as we sailed through Sag Harbor and out to the bay. What would my kids think if I really got together with Kyle? Meanwhile my phone had no service on the boat, so I couldn't even reach the kids, which sent my anxiety meter sky-high. But after some rosé, I was up dancing with the rest of the women, many of whom I'd just met.

And then "Fight Song" came on. It had been the unofficial anthem all summer, urging empowerment and owning decisions as Rachel Platten advocated.

I shed my insecurities, joined the one other woman standing on the banquette at the front of the boat as it sliced through the water, raised my hands over my head, and started belting out the lyrics. Just the way Stacey used to.

This is my fight song.

I could feel Stacey's spirit dancing through me and wondered if she knew what I was feeling. I just needed a sign.

Twenty-Four

Beach Music

"It went so fast today!"

Kyle and I walked off the court at one of our last lessons of the season.

"I know," he said, downcast. The mood had shifted. The summer traffic was ebbing again as families packed up their rafts and sandy shoes and headed back to reality.

Kyle had never done anything to pursue a real relationship with me. I was a mom, after all, not one of his tennis students or a pretty young thing he'd met out in Montauk. I had my whole life to go back to, so established that my kids' after-school fall schedules were already typed up, ready to be pinned on the family bulletin board in the city. But it was just the feeling between us that I wanted to prolong.

"Hey, I sent you a song," Kyle said as I opened the door to leave. "Listen to it today."

"A song? Really?"

"Yeah, I texted it to you. Put it on the Bluetooth in the car."

"With the kids in the car or without the kids?"

"I'm thinking without the kids," he answered. "Play it on your way home."

He walked me to my car and looked at me through the open window.

"Have a great day," he said, his elbows on the window frame. His eyes were saying what his words couldn't.

"Thank you," I whispered, looking down.

"Gotta go."

I heard him say "Heeeey, buddy!" to his next lesson. I turned the car on.

I sat in the parking lot, trying to figure out how to get the Bluetooth audio to work in my car. Which fifty-seven buttons did I have to press again? *Goddamn it!* I was sweating. My heart was pounding as I tried to get the song to play. Then, finally! A melody. I'd connected! I pulled out of the parking lot, started driving home, and pressed play.

My car, the SUV kid-mobile, with vacant car seats and boosters behind me, was suddenly filled with the sweet sounds of strumming guitar and the most beautiful voice I'd ever heard. The song was called "Famous Flower of Manhattan" by the Avett Brothers. As I drove down Route 27 in the Hamptons, past the farm stands and the workout studios and the local markets, I listened, goose bumps running up and down my arms.

> *And I found a flower in a field*
> *A field of cars and people*
> *Rows of concrete, paint and steel*
> *Manhattan is where it grew*
> *And I thought to cut it from its stem*
> *And take it from the cracks*
> *Between the bricks that it lay in*
> *And save it from the city strife*
> *Away from the city life.*

I kept listening, my eyes welling up with tears. That was how I felt. Stuck in the cracks of the city. Between immovable bricks. In need of saving. I kept driving.

Then someone they whispered in my ear
A country girl can't be made out of anybody here
Don't touch it, it loves you not
Don't touch it, it loves you not

I started crying. He was telling me how he felt. How he wasn't going to do anything. How nothing could be done and I could never be uprooted from my life. I pulled onto a side street and kept listening.

'Cause blue birds don't fly without their wings
And when we put them in a cage
The world can't hear them sing
So selfish when greed sets in
Possession, the king of sin

I was the one in a cage! That was me. I wasn't flying. But he was saying he didn't want to "possess" me either, and it was selfish of him to even try.

And people don't ever let you down
Forever find a way to kill
Whatever life they've found
A heartbeat and I want it too
Manhattan is where she grew.

He wanted my heartbeat!

So I left and I let the flower be
And yesterday I saw the flower on cable TV
Much prettier than here with me
For all of the world to see
Much prettier than here with me

The song ended. I was sobbing. I put my head on the top of the steering wheel, my shoulders heaving up and down, the tears falling into my lap. He was going to let me go. He didn't want to hurt me. He thought I'd be better off where I was, that I couldn't leave the city, couldn't leave my life. He saw me as a beautiful flower. He saw me. And I saw the tragedy of finding someone so right and yet not being able to have him.

I played the song three times, the steering wheel wet with saltwater tears, cars whizzing by me on the highway. Finally, I wiped my face. The kids were waiting. The whole thing would soon be a pleasant memory. He'd go back to teaching, meeting new women, and I'd go back to the beginning-of-school madness in the city.

But that feeling of light laughter was seductive. With Kyle, I felt like myself again. I laughed on the court. Off the court. While texting him. He brought out the part of me I thought had been lost forever. The real me. Not someone's mother. Someone's soul mate. His very presence had helped me rediscover who I was. All I had to do was listen. And blow up my life as I knew it.

Twenty-Five

Truth & Beauty

The sand slithered between our toes. After calling Kyle to thank him for the song, crying, I'd asked him to go for a walk on the beach. I was just going to lay it all on the line. If Stacey's death had taught me anything, it was that life is short. And a gift from God, a shining soul nudging into mine, shouldn't be ignored. Maybe I'd met Kyle for a reason. My mind was five hundred steps ahead.

He reached over to take my hand, and I stopped.

"Okay, look. I can't have any more kids. I had my tubes taken out when my fourth child was born. Plus I can barely handle the four I have. You don't have any of your own kids and I can't give you any. You should go out and meet some nice, pretty, young thing and go have a family. You shouldn't even think about being with me."

We stopped walking. Kyle just laughed.

"But I want to be with you," he said, smiling. "Even though you're nuts."

He hugged me from behind, the ocean in front of us, sending chills up and down my body as he touched me for the first time. "I already thought it all through. I'm all good."

"Are you sure?" I asked. "I'm telling you, I'm not worth it. Giving up kids is a huge ask. I'm really difficult. I'm not that great."

He smiled and squeezed me tighter.

"I know what I want. It's okay. And you are worth it. You're worth everything. I knew it from the first moment I touched you. I was all in. And I always will be."

———

It was time to talk to my dad, the sage counsel I spoke to before making any big life decisions. Starting a love affair with my tennis pro was something I just had to run past him. I had *Truth & Beauty* by Ann Patchett and *Cutting for Stone* by Abraham Verghese in my beach bag. As we spoke, I took notes in the endpapers.

We sat outside in the summer sun at a giant stone table overlooking the pristine lawn dotted with oak trees, Mecox Bay surrounding us on all sides.

"Dad," I said, taking a deep breath.

"Yes, Zib?"

"Dad, I've fallen in love with someone."

"You have?"

"Yes. Nothing has happened between us yet, but we've been getting to know each other and it's going to completely change my life."

"Really?"

"Really."

"Well, if nothing has happened, Zib, how could you *possibly* know this new relationship will work out?"

"I just know. I know."

"And who is this person?"

"I'm kind of afraid to tell you."

"Why?"

I took another deep breath.

"Well, actually . . . he's my tennis pro."

He just stared at me for a few long seconds, until he slowly put his head in his hands. I was hoping the fact that he loved tennis himself would help him overlook how bad this appeared.

Nope.

Months later, when I told another family friend, the response was: "What, the gardener was taken?"

Twenty-Six

BLUSH

C an you meet up? I just left my dad's."

"I'm all sweaty from teaching a few lessons, but sure."

I waited in my car in the parking lot in town. When Kyle pulled up next to me in his small black sedan, I jumped in. He was drenched with sweat and very smelly from tennis. I didn't care. The tension was palpable. It was Labor Day weekend, and we were running out of time.

"Hey," he said softly.

"Hey," I said. "I just told my dad about you."

"Yeah? How'd that go?"

"Um . . ."

He laughed.

"To be honest, he couldn't believe I was so sure we'd be good together if we hadn't, you know, *been* together."

"You talk to your dad about that stuff?!"

"I do. I know. Is that weird?"

Slowly, Kyle reached out his hand and lightly touched my leg. He started rubbing my thigh a little as we both watched his hand move. Then I turned my head toward his as he looked at me, deep into my eyes. And we leaned forward and kissed.

Holy fucking shit.

Our lips fit together like pieces of a puzzle, like we'd been sculpted by God explicitly to be with each other. We kissed with passion and intensity, stopping every so often to hug each other tightly as if we were on an ice floe drifting at sea with only each other to steady ourselves.

My body lit up. I'd never felt such an electric, chemical, spiritual connection. The first kiss likely lasted only two minutes, but it was utterly and completely life-changing.

We pulled away from each other.

"Holy shit," he said.

"Wow."

"A-MAZ-ing!"

He looked at me.

"Are you sure about this?"

"Yes!"

He looked at the clock on the dashboard.

"I have a lesson in five minutes. I'll call you after?"

We kissed again.

"Let's meet on the beach tonight."

I hopped out of his car and got back into mine. My hands were shaking. I couldn't drive; I just sat there in the parking lot, my cheeks flushed. I wanted to scream at the top of my lungs with excitement: I JUST KISSED KYLE!

But what was I DOING?! I had four kids! I couldn't be kissing my tennis pro in a parking lot like I was in some movie.

I knew it wasn't the way that it seemed on paper. I'd discovered my soul mate. But still.

———

Later that night, I got the kids to bed, left them with Tenzin, and packed a black woven beach bag with towels, wine, plastic cups, a corkscrew, and candles. I wore a long, sleeveless, flowered Tory Burch dress with wedge cork heels, and I drove away from the house feeling guilty and excited all at once.

"You look amazing," Kyle said when we got out of our cars. He whistled. I beamed. I *felt* amazing. He was wearing jeans and a black T-shirt.

"I brought blankets."

He reached into his car and pulled out a ratty brown chenille blanket from what looked like the 1970s.

"I don't even want to know where that thing has been," I said.

He laughed his hearty, guttural laugh.

"Let's use mine."

I could feel the cool sand on the bottoms of my feet. I could hear the sound of the water lapping under the starry sky, whooshing in and out. I could see the deserted beach, empty aside from the shifting dunes, the footsteps of scampering kids—now sleeping soundly in their matching pajamas—etched deeply into the sand.

"How about here?"

We laid down my blanket. We never opened the tote bag.

I hadn't hooked up with someone on a beach since the mid-nineties. I felt completely self-conscious at first. My body was a wreck after four children. Later, I warned Kyle about my stomach so many times that eventually he said, "Let me just see what we're dealing with here." And he'd kissed the scars from my three C-sections.

We kissed, but mostly we snuggled together that evening, my head fitting perfectly under his chin, as we talked and laughed under the stars.

"What?"

"I can't believe we're doing this!"

"Same here!"

Kyle made me laugh harder than I had in years, poking fun at the craziness of my life in a hilarious, good-natured way.

"Are you always this funny?" I asked at one point.

"Yes!"

Before we got back into our cars, we clung to each other, kissing like lovesick kids under the black starry sky, sand on our feet, our hair windblown. Eyes ablaze.

He called me when I got home to make sure I was home safe.

"So this is it, right? You're in?" I asked.

"I'm in."

Kyle later told me he hung up the phone and fell back on his bed. He looked up at the ceiling, smiling, and thought, "Okay, I guess this is really happening."

D

2015–2018

Twenty-Seven

World Travel

Bienvenidos a Miami.

Kyle's and my first trip together was to South Florida. I was a bit nervous. At close to forty, married and divorced, I was pretty set in my ways. But Kyle had booked the trip and the room, and he had missed a friend's wedding just to be alone with me. My bags were packed. I was ready to try to go with the flow.

After we checked in at the airport, instead of waiting by the gate, ready to board thirty minutes early like I usually did, Kyle said, "Hey, let's go get a drink!"

A drink? At the airport?

"Do we have enough time?"

He laughed.

"Honey, we have plenty of time. We've got nothing *but* time! Come on."

Instead of guarding our place in the boarding line, we walked to the restaurant and sat at the bar drinking beer (beer!) until the flight was called. Not only that, we weren't the first ones on the plane.

"What's the rush?" Kyle asked. "We'll all get there at the same time."

This went against my what-if-my-overhead-bag-doesn't-fit agita. But I went with it. Maybe I could be more laid-back. I mean, I could try.

Kyle and I couldn't keep our hands off each other on the airplane. The plastic armrest suddenly felt insurmountable. I actually sat on Kyle's lap and snuggled with him for a while until the flight attendant made me sit in my own seat. I didn't pull out a book. I didn't watch a movie. We just talked and laughed and cuddled.

By the time we got to the One Hotel in Miami, which Kyle had booked for us online, I felt like a teenager. The hotel lobby had a cool vibe, lots of reclaimed wood and plants and comfy couches. We dropped our bags next to the low, loft-style bed in the room and walked over to the window. Our view was of a garbage dump in an alleyway.

"Oh no," Kyle exclaimed. "They said it was ocean view!"

"Well, wait, look," I replied, smooshing my face on the glass. "If you press your nose up against the glass, you can see the ocean! See? A tiny speck of blue."

"This is my view," Kyle said, hugging me. "This is what I want to look at."

Normally I would have changed rooms. Twice. This time, I didn't say a word.

———

As we got ready to head to the beach the first morning, Kyle was wearing his tennis shorts and a T-shirt.

"Oh no! Did you forget to pack a bathing suit?"

"This is what I swim in. It's all good."

"But wouldn't you rather change into a suit?"

"Actually"—he paused—"I don't have a bathing suit."

"You don't have a bathing suit?"

"No. I don't usually swim that much."

"But you go to the beach all the time! Have you *ever* had a bathing suit?"

"Yes! I had bathing suits as a kid. But honestly, I haven't had much time off in the past twelve years. Maybe a day or two here or there. I usually teach tennis seven days a week. I haven't been going on vacations like this. So it hasn't been a big deal."

"Oh, okay."

"Ready to go?"

He grabbed my hand and we left the room.

———

We talked on the beach about our career goals. Kyle had gotten another job teaching tennis in the city and had upended his entire life to be with me, but he was still trying to figure out how to pursue his dream of being in the entertainment industry. I wasn't sure how he was going to transition from tennis into, well, anything, but he didn't seem worried.

"Honey, I know you're saying your tennis career is almost over, but how *exactly* are you going to find the next thing? How can you just break into entertainment? That's, like, impossible."

"Don't worry," he said, reaching over to grab my hand. "I've got this. It'll all unfold organically, as it should."

Having spent most of my type-A life focused on and planning for what was coming next—college, job, grad school, job—the idea that an entire career would just suddenly unfold seemed hard to swallow.

I sighed.

Kyle looked me in the eye.

"Trust me. I've got this."

———

The previous week on East Eighty-Third Street (just a few blocks from Lyle the Crocodile!), I had gone to a girls' dinner with school moms at a Mexican restaurant. As I told them about getting together with Kyle, the eight moms all leaned forward over their margaritas, rapt, hanging on every word of my story. When the waiter came over in the middle, one of them yelled, "Not now!"

One girlfriend, Nancy, took me aside on the street afterward.

"So you really think this is it? This guy?"

"Oh yeah," I replied. "We're going to get married!"

"What?" she'd said, laughing. "Are you crazy?"

"I'm serious! Trust me. Watch and see. We even know what rings we want!"

She looked at me skeptically.

It wasn't just her. Most of my friends thought I'd gone insane.

I'd also told Paige, my Kentucky mom friend from ballet and pre-school who had beaten ovarian cancer, about Kyle early on. She had been an ardent supporter of my newfound happiness and super nice to Kyle. She had even asked me to send her videos of what his first seder was like so she could laugh along with him as a fellow Catholic. The four of us had just attended a benefit together, sitting side by side over dinner as another member of our Breakfast Club was honored.

In Miami with Kyle, I was reading Emily Giffin's *Something Borrowed* on the beach when I got a text from Paige. She'd had a little fever after some gallbladder surgery and wasn't it nuts but she was actually at Memorial Sloan Kettering again. When I asked her if it was cancer, she said all the blood tests had come back negative so far but that I should keep praying. I offered to take her daughter, as I had many times during her earlier go-round with cancer, but with the girls at different schools, she didn't need my help; her enormous support group at her daughter's new school had stepped up.

But maybe I shouldn't have taken a girls' trip to Palm Beach last week after all, she wrote. Not feeling like myself. Oh well!

———

Over that first weekend in Miami I noticed Kyle didn't have any clothes that weren't for playing tennis, aside from jeans. We hadn't talked about finances before, but it was becoming clear that we'd grown up and were living quite differently.

Kyle often told me he made "good money" from his tennis career and that he had everything he could ever want, enough to give back to his friends and family. He felt beyond grateful.

"I don't need a thing," he said. "I have everything I need."

Gift giving was going to be a cinch.

Kyle often felt uncomfortable when we did things like take the complimentary limo in Vegas that the casino provided on our trip there. When we got to the valet area at the hotel, Kyle greeted the limo driver we'd had once before by shouting, "Bud-DYYY! You're back! Good to see ya, man!" And then he went over to hug him. The door attendants didn't know how to respond.

"He gets very excited," I told them as they watched Kyle embrace the driver.

He asked everyone questions, something we had in common.

"How's your day going?" he asked the bartender. "Easy night?"

"What'd you do last weekend?" he asked the waiter at the golf club. "Come sit with us!"

"Come on, honey," he'd say. "Everyone has a story. Everyone should be asked how their day was, no matter what role they're playing in life. We're all just people. Being professional by keeping a distance? Nah."

On the beach at the One Hotel that first getaway weekend in Miami, we talked in more detail about our childhoods. He couldn't believe how lucky I was, but he felt just as lucky himself, especially having been raised by "the most amazing family ever." We held hands on a double lounge-chair on the beach and shared our life stories. I read

Amor Towles's *Rules of Civility* and Will Schwalbe's *The End of Your Life Book Club* between our heart-to-hearts.

Who cared that he hadn't heard of the musical *Hamilton*? So what that he didn't know what "Art Basel" was until we attended the art fair where he picked out a gorgeous pink photo for our new living room. And he truly didn't understand all the fancy charity dinners we went to.

"How are they raising money if they're throwing this huge party?" (Good point!)

He almost fainted when I took him to the Vilebrequin bathing suit store and he saw the price tags. (Now the salesman at the Vilebrequin store on Madison knows him by name.) Being with Kyle made me see everything about my crazy life in New York with new eyes. His favorite TV show was Jill Kargman's *Odd Mom Out*, based on her hilarious book *Momzillas*. He felt like it was about him. He couldn't believe I'd actually grown up with Jill. Or that everyone we met on the street seemed to have known me since I was a kid.

"I'm still in touch with one person, Wally, from when I was little," he said. "Every coffee shop we go to, every time we go anywhere, someone else tells me they went to preschool with you! This is nuts!"

I laughed.

"A lot of native New Yorkers just stay in New York," I said. "It's actually a really small town here on the Upper East Side." Soon, he was its newest resident.

Twenty-Eight

JULIE & JULIA

"What are you up to, love?"

I was at Kyle's new apartment in the city, which we called The Nest (like the book), working on my computer at the kitchen table. Kyle was sitting on the sofa, hunched over his laptop on the glass coffee table, his brow furrowed.

"Well, I'm trying to figure out how to launch a Kickstarter campaign."

"A Kickstarter campaign? Why?"

"My mom and sister want to take their local baking business and turn it into a full-on company. I thought I could help them by raising the money on Kickstarter to get it off the ground."

"Wait, wait, wait, wait. Tell me more."

"They've been thinking about it for a while, but now they're ready to do it. They make all these amazing desserts and sell them locally, but the one that everyone raves about is my grandmother Nene's crumb cake. Maybe they can start selling just the crumb cake more widely."

I love starting businesses. There's something that I find intoxicating about taking an idea and branding it, finding the right audience, and getting it off the ground. An opportunity for a new business right here in The Nest? Sign me up!

Kyle's grandmother Nene, an eighty-six-year-old New Jersey native and Charleston transplant, had been making her famous crumb cake for sixty years. The thick crumb-to-cake ratio, the rich buttery taste of the crumbs, and the delicious, moist cake made it irresistible—and addictive.

I first tried it when a group of girlfriends and I went down to Charleston. His mom, Susan, had dropped off a care package for me at the hotel; it included a crumb cake, crumb truffles, plastic forks and napkins, and a bottle of Prosecco, all packaged in a woven basket with a ribbon. I would meet Susan in person the next morning, but by that point I had spent hours on the phone with her. I stood over the box, shoveling the crumb topping into my mouth like a starved animal. I couldn't put my fork down.

"How much are you trying to raise?" I asked that night. "And what for?"

"I don't know exactly," Kyle responded. "I'm just trying to get it started."

"Let's get your mom on the phone," I said, closing my laptop. "Maybe I can help."

The next thing they knew, I was whipping up a business plan, projecting revenues and expenses, commissioning a logo, hiring a lawyer, applying for a trademark, getting an accountant, forming an LLC, and developing a marketing/PR plan. I brainstormed the name of the business with Kyle and his family and then worked with them on corporate identity. I crafted the tagline: *You won't leave a crumb.*

Any free time I had between kid drop-offs and pickups, I threw into Nene's Treats. I used all my parenting and personal connections to help them get distribution, advice, and press, and even invested in the business myself before introducing them to other potential investors. In fact, it was a former babysitter who got Nene's Treats into Butterfield Market, the local gourmet store on Seventy-Seventh and Lexington. Susan, Nene, and Stefanie, Kyle's sister, who helped with the entire business and the baking, were shocked and delighted. I was relieved to know that I'd finally gotten use out of something I'd learned in business school.

Along the way, I also became a logistics manager. The cakes stayed fresh for only a few days after they were baked. How could we get them to stores across the country before they went bad? Luckily, they froze very well. The challenge became transporting them and storing them frozen. I started learning more about shipping frozen goods and logistics management than I'd ever wanted to know before. I was interviewing competitive "ROFR" (refrigerated and freezer) trucks and frozen storage facilities, calling business school classmates who could help. Kyle even toured a facility in New Jersey, sending me pictures of himself making a thumbs-up sign in front of a giant polar bear.

A new, huge order came in from Whole Foods. We couldn't figure out how to produce enough cakes to fulfill their order. I spent an afternoon on a call presenting Nene's Treats to all the catering managers at a national hotel chain. I was also trying to help with the stringent label requirements, the Fancy Food Show, the boxes. I spoke to an Orthodox Jewish man who pulled out his selection of pastry box samples in the middle of Butterfield Market, and then I mistakenly ordered tens of thousands of boxes because I didn't realize I'd ordered in bulk. A moving truck pulled up to Kyle's mom's driveway in Charleston with a forklift.

For marketing, Kyle and I did extensive sampling. As soon as potential customers tried the crumb cake, they bought it. We just had to find people to keep trying it. We worked at benefits, farm stands, and grocery stores, as did Kyle's mom and sister in the South. Sometimes the kids joined, although the samples suspiciously disappeared before anyone else could taste them. I made banners, signs, and handouts. We met with private equity food investors, mostly friends of friends of mine from business school; we also had one meeting at Pinnacle Foods, complete with the Vlasic pickle bird statue greeting us at the front door.

Everyone in my family got involved to help. Gagy and her best friend, Marilyn, got us into a high-end grocery store in Dayton, Ohio. My mom sat next to Florence Fabricant, a food writer at the *New York Times*, at the hair salon and pitched the topic to her. Nene's Treats was mentioned a few weeks later in the Food section. Everyone was buzzing.

And I was getting fat.

By the end of the first few months of constant testing and sampling, I couldn't fit into my jeans. Forget my jeans: even my pajamas were getting snug. But I was excited and energized; Kyle and I were doing something together, building something new, embarking on a creative endeavor.

A friend helped us get a booth at her preschool's fair, where every tall, skinny woman who walked by would say, "Oh my God, I shouldn't! I couldn't!" Then many would circle back and take our smallest "mini," saying, "I'll just give this to my daughter later." I gave them out at all my board meetings. In charity goodie bags. At school events. We had crumbs coming out of our ears. Susan and Stefanie didn't sleep for months, baking and packaging around the clock at a commercial kitchen to meet the demand from all the stores. The shipping costs were proving to be much higher than I'd budgeted for in my initial spreadsheet, throwing off all my estimates. In a meeting with my dad, he was quick to point out that it looked like I had forgotten tax costs.

We started interviewing different co-packers (factories) to make more crumb cakes. Kyle's mom and sister would send us pictures of them in caps and robes, *Laverne & Shirley* style, testing out various production facilities. But nothing tasted as good as the ones they baked themselves. I read *Sweetbitter* by Stephanie Danler and *Modern Lovers* by Emma Straub at night, taking a break from the business. I took notes on *Lean In* by Sheryl Sandberg.

Eventually, we decided to migrate sales away from retail to exclusively online. A company called Goldbelly would take care of the dreaded shipping. With just Susan and Stefanie, it was impossible to fulfill the giant Whole Foods order, and a later one from QVC. We had to pass, despite the hours I'd spent on the phone and filling out forms to partner up with UNFI, a natural foods distributor.

I tried to do a lot of this work from home, but it was getting harder and harder. I'd be on a call with a shipping firm while wandering in and out of the playroom, the kids clamoring for my attention. The crumb cake was so good, so specific, so tangible, that even the kids were into the business, but not when it got in the way of a round of hide-and-seek.

As the business expanded, I couldn't spend enough time with the kids and still do my "job" at the level I expected of myself or the company needed at that stage. My wonderful relationship with Susan and Stefanie, which I'd basically formed over the phone dealing with the business, threatened to become strained because I couldn't accomplish my set of tasks on time. After a lot of deliberation, I decided to step down from my official CEO role in the business and handed it all back over to Susan, who had been running the operations all along.

The best was what came out of it for me: a close relationship with my future in-laws, gratitude from Kyle for helping his family, intellectual stimulation, and overall excitement. I couldn't wait to see where the business would go next. But from the sidelines. I still needed to fit into those jeans, after all.

Eventually, Susan and Stefanie found a co-packer to make the cakes and began selling on Goldbelly. Kyle started calling me "Crumbdog millionaire."

———

I was cochairing the Library Lunch at the New York Public Library when a text came in from a Breakfast Club mom. I had just given a speech in the giant rotunda, gorgeous purple-and-white centerpieces framed by piles of books lining the dozens of round tables, matrons and young women filling in every nook of the massive room to hear a panel of authors speak.

Did you hear about Paige?

I texted back under the table.

No. Is everything okay?

The cancer is back. There's a prayer service happening this weekend. Want to go?

Oh no! I'll be out of town. What happened?

Paige's cancer had returned and had spread everywhere. Her liver was shutting down. She had taken her kids out of school and was holed up at a friend's house in Locust Valley. I couldn't believe it. I still held out hope and prayed on my own.

Twenty-Nine

MALIBU RISING

Kyle fell in love at first sight, but not with me. He stepped through the sliding airport doors and swooned over Los Angeles. The view. The palm trees. The climate. The relaxed people. The vibe. The ocean breeze.

It was another one of our early trips. I wanted to visit my brother and his family who lived there.

"Ho-NEY!" he said, getting into our Uber. "I feel like I'm home!"

By the time we got to the Loews hotel in Santa Monica that first trip and were settling into our corner room with a view of the ocean and the setting sun, Kyle was absolutely infatuated.

"Okay, can we please move here?" he asked. "This is amazing. This place is a dream come true! Look at it!"

He pointed out the window. It was pretty awesome: the miles of sand, the lapping waves, the bicyclists circling by, the sunshine.

"No, we can't move here," I responded, shaking my head. "Uh, the kids, remember?"

"They have schools in LA, too!"

"We're not all moving here. But I love it, too. Let's just spend as much time here as we can."

Watching Kyle drive our rental car, his left hand on the top of the wheel, arm outstretched, his right hand holding mine, made me flash back to our limited time together in the Hamptons. Kyle just loved driving. He'd given his car to his parents in Charleston when he moved to New York and had felt a bit adrift ever since. In LA, he could be in control. Navigate.

I was happier out there, too. I could start over. As we explored the city, doing a studio tour at Warner Brothers, eating at cool restaurants in Venice, having brunch at Farmshop in Brentwood, getting sushi at Katsuya, and devouring marble cake at SusieCakes bakery, we laughed and smiled and ate and rested.

———

I was at the Hotel Bel-Air on an elliptical machine, John Legend on the one next to me, when a text came in from Tripp. Paige had just passed away. He texted a group of us: She was saying, "I love you, I love you, I love you," to the kids until the moment she died.

The pedals sank to the floor as I burst into tears. I hopped off, ran out of the gym, and called our mutual friend from beneath the curtain of verdant trees.

"She's gone, Zibs. I can't believe it."

My friend and I cried together, across the country, as I tried to process the news.

"But her five kids! Tripp!"

"I know. She was with them at the end. I heard from Tripp that she got all your texts, everyone's, and smiled as he read them all out loud to her, but she didn't want to take time away from her kids to respond."

I hung up the phone and stood there, sobbing, while the famous swans of the storied Bel-Air hotel slowly swam upstream. Later that day in Malibu, I walked along the rocky beach, the sand under my toes, talking to the rest of our crew. How could it be? It seemed impossible. And I felt so very far away. Alone.

———

After LA, Kyle and I sat with the Group Six Breakfast Club at St. James' Church for Paige's memorial service, held at 11:11 a.m., the time of day when she always felt surrounded by angels. Fitting that I was in the City of Angels when we lost her. I wore leopard-print shoes to the service.

Paige and I were close friends for seven years, but her spirit still feels like it's everywhere. Three years later, on another trip to LA, I had a session with a medium, Vickie Emanuele, and asked her about Paige.

Vickie's whole posture changed and, suddenly in Paige's characteristic drawl, she said, "Well, she is just *thrilled* that you thought about her!" She said Paige was watching over her many kids and was at peace, that she was just so "touched" I was keeping her in my thoughts. Vickie told me, "She wants you to be happy, to celebrate. She's saying 'Cheers!' She wants you to party. I keep hearing her say, 'Party hard. Party hardy. Party hardy'?"

"Oh my gosh. The Hardy Party. That's what she called her family. That's how she signed her holiday cards. All of it."

"Yes, Hardy Party. She says, 'Cheers!'"

Not only that, but Vickie heard from Stacey, who was over-the-moon excited about how happy I was with Kyle.

I knew she would be.

I knew she was.

Thirty

THE HAPPINESS PROJECT

It became a family affair. I finally introduced Kyle to the kids. I didn't want to rush into that until everything was completely set in stone with Kyle and any growing pains had been worked out.

I loved looking out the kitchen window in the Hamptons while doing the dishes and seeing him chase the little guys around the yard, cheer on my older daughter as she cartwheeled, or throw a football with my son. Just having Kyle around made life more fun. The kids could sense my new energy. And they instantly adored him.

"Mom, you're so smiley with Kyle all the time," my son said one night as I was putting him to bed.

"I'm really happy," I responded. "I'm glad you noticed!"

But then, the zingers.

"When are you going to go back to *your* house?" my little girl asked Kyle one evening.

"Why are you always here?" my daughter asked.

"Where are *your* kids?" added my son.

Kyle always had a funny response ready, unflustered.

"I'm leaving right now," he'd say. Or "I'm just here to hang out with your awesome mom." Even "Why are *you* still here?"

I read *The Happiness Project* by Gretchen Rubin and Charles Duhigg's *The Power of Habit*, and I enjoyed the summer break. When Kyle moved in, the kids thought it was so funny to see his clothes hanging in the downstairs closet, like props for a play.

Kyle had adjustments to make. He had to face deep disappointment after cooking a delicious meal for the whole family, only to have the kids take one bite and ask for chicken nuggets.

One evening, he spent hours making a sensational chicken teriyaki with rice and broccoli, but the kids weren't used to so many flavors. They refused to eat it. They liked their broccoli simply steamed with a little butter—or not at all. They took one look at their plates and started freaking out: "I don't like this dinner!"

Kyle stood at the stove, dirty pans on three burners, silver mixing bowls all around him, tongs haphazardly discarded nearby. He was sweating from all the cooking, and the pressure to have it ready at exactly 6:00 p.m., because "they eat at 6:00 p.m.!" It was the only time I thought they might break his spirit.

"Honey, I love the dinner," I said, coming over to hug him. "Don't worry about the kids. They'll get used to your cooking."

He smiled weakly.

During the pandemic, Kyle cooked us all three meals a day. I read Jessica Seinfeld's *Deceptively Delicious*, Gwyneth Paltrow's *It's All Easy*, and Julia Turshen's cookbook *Simply Julia*, and gave Kyle some suggestions.

———

One morning Kyle woke up, still sleepy after his battle with insomnia the night before. He made himself an espresso and a cup of dark roast coffee and padded over to the couch in his sleep shorts and T-shirt to watch the SportsCenter highlights.

I came rushing through the room, having been up for hours already.

"Wait! No TV! Please!"

"What?" he asked sleepily. "Why not?"

"Please, if the kids see the TV on, they'll . . ."

Next thing I knew, my two daughters had seen the flicker of the TV light, thrown themselves on the couch, and started screaming.

"*Paw Patrol*! I want *Paw Patrol*! Can I, Mama? Can I?"

"*Ninja Warrior*! Can I watch *Ninja Warrior*? Please?"

Kyle sat back and sank into the cushion.

"No TV, guys!" I said. "No TV!"

"But, Ma-maaaa!"

I just looked at Kyle.

"Got it," he said, holding both hands up in the air like he was at gunpoint. "Point taken."

———

Connie, my mom's housekeeper, was a youthful-looking, sprightly forty-nine. By the time I had twin nine-year-olds, a three-year-old, and a one-year-old, she'd been with my family for thirty years. Instrumental when I was on bed rest, she used to come over to visit the kids frequently. She'd play on the floor with them whenever we visited my mom or chase them through the hallway that circled through the apartment.

After work one afternoon, Connie was waiting for the subway in Times Square on her way to visit a friend who was expecting a baby. As the train charged into the station, a schizophrenic woman, recently released from Bellevue Hospital, pushed Connie in front of it.

We believe she died on impact.

Howard called to tell me. I was pushing the stroller down the street, paused to take the call, and almost vomited. I couldn't stop shaking. I ran home, pushing the stroller at superspeed, the kids howling with delight at my sprinting when all I wanted to do was collapse inside.

I was no stranger to trauma and sudden death, but another senseless murder? Connie!

I couldn't take it.

As I mourned Connie, taking calls from reporters at the *New York Post* and nursing my own sorrow, I read *The Last Lecture* by Randy Pausch and *The Middle Place* by Kelly Corrigan.

Connie lived to make other people happy. That was all she wanted. I flashed back to all the ways she had taken care of me, every holiday she had been a part of. Her wedding. Now another loved one had been instantly snatched away by the cruel hands of fate. Another reminder of how unfair and random life could be. Every day I avoided death's clutches was a win.

The woman who pushed Connie was sent to prison, where she later hanged herself.

I still look for Connie whenever I walk into my mom's apartment, expecting to hear her voice calling from just around the corner. Kyle and I went to yet another funeral together.

When we stopped by the wake in New Jersey at Connie's husband's family's house, I hugged her husband tightly.

"Please let me know if there's anything I can do," I said, looking him in the eye.

He shuffled on his feet.

"Well, to tell you the truth, our apartment's getting pretty messy. Connie always did such a great job of straightening it up. Would you mind coming by and doin' a little cleaning? Maybe grab some garbage bags?"

"Mark! Are you crazy!" his mom yelled from the couch, the rest of the relatives erupting in laughter. "Zibby's not coming to clean your house!"

"Hey, if you need it, I'm there," I said.

I thought of one of my recent SoulCycle classes, when the instructor, Mireya D'Angelo, was talking about the importance of "recovering." And "recovery" could be interpreted in many ways. I was recovering in every way, not just in my soul, but also in my wardrobe. Kyle encouraged me to be more daring, to wear brighter colors, higher shoes, to relax in a pair of sweatpants instead of jeans. Over Labor Day weekend at the end of that summer, a full year after being together, Kyle pulled me onto the upstairs terrace in the Water Mill home.

"Watch us have a catch," he said, dragging my son with him.

"On the balcony? Don't have a catch on the balcony!" I scolded. "The ball will fly over the side!"

"It'll be fine. Come on," Kyle said. "Actually, all the kids can watch us. Come on out, guys!"

The three others materialized as if he'd just whistled like in *The Sound of Music*. They ran past me onto the balcony, smiling mischievously. Kyle and my son kept throwing a baseball back and forth until, during one throw, something else flew through the air.

Kyle exclaimed, "Hey, what's that?"

Then he got down on one knee, surrounded by all four kids, and opened the box to reveal the gorgeous ring inside. He looked me in the eye and asked, "Will you marry me?"

The kids started screaming with excitement. I covered my mouth with both hands and then screamed, too.

"Yes!" I answered, jumping up and down. "Yes, yes!"

Kyle got up and hugged me and the kids all came running toward us and hugged us, too. My son called out, "Group hug!" It was beautiful and perfect.

What a catch.

Thirty-One

THE BIG FINISH

Of course, my bridal shower was a "book shower." My mom, Gen, and other friends knew there was nothing I loved doing more than reading. Everyone brought me a book they loved, inscribed. Susan, my future mother-in-law, dealt with five hours of flight delays and a day off from baking crumb cakes around the clock to be there.

I couldn't believe my good fortune. The home, the love, the books.

Kyle and I lay beside each other on the couch later that evening, our heads at opposite ends, the books from the shower tucked away on the shelves surrounding us. He was rubbing my feet as he watched football and I read Daphne Merkin's *This Close to Happy*. I'd recently finished Celeste Ng's new book *Little Fires Everywhere* and had begged Kyle to go to a literary lunch at Amici in Brentwood with me to meet her. The previous trip to LA, I'd asked him to come with me to a breakfast for Dani Shapiro after we saw her read from *Hourglass* at Diesel bookstore.

Out of nowhere, Kyle said, "I'm thinking of converting to Judaism."

The book fell on my chest.

"Really? You would think about doing that?"

Kyle had grown up Catholic. His father wore a cross around his neck. Susan started planning her Christmas dinner menu right after Easter. Meanwhile, I had grown up Jewish. We celebrated Shabbat most

Fridays, a custom my former in-laws modeled for me. The kids went to Hebrew school. Kyle and I would go with the twins to *tefilah*, the prayer service at the end of Hebrew school each week. Kyle would sing the prayers, reading the words on the screen intended for the kids, soaking it all in. Years later, the twins would have separate bar and bat mitzvahs on Zoom during the pandemic. Kyle even tolerated it when I begged a hotel concierge in Las Vegas to rummage up a challah a few hours before sundown.

My maternal grandmother Gagy's second husband, Papa Kal, had been a rabbi before he passed away. She almost fainted with excitement when I told her Kyle was converting.

"Oh for goodness' sake," she said. "Isn't that lovely? He's a mensch! I wish Kal were here to see it."

My other grandparents, all deceased, would have appreciated it, too.

Kyle said he felt like he was Jewish already because he'd watched every single episode of *Seinfeld*. His family thought it was a beautiful, generous act of love that he wanted to convert for the kids and me and supported him every step of the way.

Kyle said, "If there is an afterlife, I want to make sure we're going to the same place." (We'd like to have our ashes mixed in a shared jar so we can be together for all eternity.)

I introduced Kyle to the rabbi at our local temple, Rabbi Gelfand. Kyle loved to listen to the rabbi's long explanations of Jewish history and culture, sprinkled with stories about where the rabbi got his shirts made.

Knowing that Kyle was more of a visual learner than a reader, the rabbi assigned Kyle piles of old DVDs to watch. Kyle would come back from his sessions holding a tattered case of *Fiddler on the Roof* or *Schindler's List*, even old favorites like *Crossing Delancey* or *The Chosen*.

One dreary Saturday afternoon, we got in bed to watch *Fiddler on the Roof*. About halfway through, I fell asleep with my head on Kyle's arm, nuzzled into his chest. His arm fell asleep in its trapped position as he watched the credits roll on the screen.

"Huh, the Jews didn't have it too bad," Kyle thought to himself, a bit confused by the ending.

Pinned down and not wanting to disturb my sleep, Kyle just lay there watching the credits, his eyes closing. Suddenly, he heard talking and sat up a bit to check out the screen. He wondered what was going on and quickly checked the movie's run time with his free hand.

That was intermission! He was only halfway done.

Kyle even completed the required "mikvah" custom by getting into a sacred hot tub on the Upper West Side and accepting his new Jewish responsibilities. The rabbi; Kyle's dad; and my stepdad, Howard, met us there. We marched down the tiled hallway as if we were in a spa while Kyle changed. Then, away from our prying eyes, he lowered himself into the sacred water. The rabbi asked him three questions with the advance heads-up that the answers would all be "yes," and that was it.

"Mazel tov!"

Kyle's dad started crying.

"I'm just so proud of you, Ky," his dad said, hugging him. "It's such a beautiful thing that you did."

At the temple's Shabbat services shortly before our wedding, Kyle got up at the bimah and made a speech about how excited he was to be a member of the tribe, especially to join our family. Then the kids and I went onstage to welcome him. The little kids kept poking each other and laughing. I felt like the entire universe had conspired to give me this holy gift.

Afterward, I threw him a conversion party. The Paperless Post, on a matzoh background, announced: "Oy! Kyle's converting! Please join us for Chinese food to welcome the newest member of the tribe." I served Shun Lee Chinese food family style. People sat all over the apartment: on the floor, on the kitchen counter, everywhere. Shoes off. His family mingling with our friends and family. Friends bought him *Great Jews in Sports* by Robert Slater and *The New Jewish Wedding* by Anita Diamant.

Kyle's conversion came just before the spike in anti-Semitism, the anti-Israel sentiment, and the attacks on Jews at the Tree of Life synagogue in Pittsburgh and elsewhere.

"Bad timing, love," I joked recently while reading the horrific news in the paper. "Sorry about that."

He just shrugged.

"We're in it together."

Thirty-Two

LOVE POEMS FOR MARRIED PEOPLE

Love, all.

We got married on the tennis court in the backyard of a rental home in Water Mill, right below the balcony where we'd gotten engaged. The rehearsal dinner was the evening before at the same beach club where I'd introduced the kids to Kyle. My children, my nieces and nephew from LA, and Gen's kids frolicked like puppies in the sand. They jumped off the lifeguard chair, the girls' matching hot-pink party dresses opening up like umbrellas as they leaped. Harry, the owner of the nearby farm stand that had sold Nene's Treats for us, surprised us with an extra-large challah.

Kyle and I posed barefoot for pictures on the sand, my head on his shoulder, him kissing the top of my head. I wore a navy-blue dress with tennis rackets embroidered on it from Ann Taylor. Kyle's and my families intermingled, many meeting for the first time, marveling at our match. His friends, mostly musicians and athletes, delighted my more conservative friends from the private school, Ivy League set I'd grown up in.

Gagy pulled aside Kyle's best friend, Don.

"You know you'd look a lot more handsome without that beard. Don't you own a brush? Can I comb your hair a little?"

When we told Don that Gagy had passed away recently, at age ninety-seven, he cried.

I never got a chance to say goodbye to Gagy in person because she passed away during Covid when I was too afraid to fly. Another medium, Laura Lynne Jackson, author of *Signs*, told me that Gagy had barged right in to our podcast interview ("a little pushy, actually") to tell me not to worry about saying goodbye. That it meant nothing and she knew how much I loved her. She also said she was there for an anniversary of some sort. I couldn't think of what it could be. After we spoke, I went downstairs and opened a gift-wrapped box my mom had dropped off. It was Gagy's ashes.

———

Susan and Stefanie got ready for the wedding with the girls and me, having our hair done and our makeup carefully applied. Kyle's two good friends, Mike and Dan from the band Dangermuffin, came over to rehearse the song they would sing for us at the reception, their priceless gift. I heard music coming from the basement and stopped, mid-hair-styling, to run down to check it out. On the landing I met Kyle, who'd also heard it.

"What's that music?" I asked.

"Shh, they're rehearsing. Let's check it out."

We tiptoed down the stairs, holding hands, and saw Mike and Dan on guitars, along with Don, who was singing "Sweet Baby James." It gave me chills. The soothing sounds of the melody. The guitar chords hitting the walls of the empty basement. Don's beautiful singing voice. The song. The intensity. The intimacy. Just the three of them, Kyle's best friends, and the two of us, being serenaded on the stairs. It was magical.

Before the ceremony, Rabbi Gelfand led our immediate families and us in a ketubah signing ceremony. I felt particularly connected to Kyle's mom, Susan, bedecked in a gorgeous green dress, whose kind eyes welled with tears as she spoke of our happiness. It was her sixtieth birthday that night and we celebrated with a cake for her beside our wedding cake.

My sons walked down the aisle together in navy suits, light-blue button-downs, and old-school Adidas sneakers, carrying lunch boxes that read "Ring Security." My daughters followed in flowing white sleeveless dresses with silvery circles sewn into the crinoline of the skirts. They carried a sign that read "The Bride Is on Her Way."

Kyle and I read each other handwritten vows. We circled the chuppah with the kids and attempted the Jewish custom of seven circles, but after one I declared, "Okay, that's enough."

As we exchanged rings, I couldn't help but shiver thinking of how far we'd come. Now we were outside in the sunshine, out in the open, getting married in front of friends, family, and God.

At the end, Kyle stomped on the glass as my daughter called out, "Mazel tov!" There's a slow-motion video someone took of me that night, in the middle of all the festivities, surrounded by people during cocktail hour, spinning around, my skirt making a halo around me as I slowly turned, beaming, laughing. I was so close to never feeling that happiness. And yet, somehow, it had found me. The flower from Manhattan.

Susan cut her cake, also beaming and laughing, her long brunette hair glistening like she had just stepped out of a salon, as Nene looked on proudly. Gagy smiled the whole night. My girlfriend Nancy, who had seemed skeptical when I vowed that Kyle and I would end up married after that girls' dinner, held my hand and laughed as we danced the horah.

My silver Vans peeked out from under my strapless princess dress all night.

We gave everyone a Nene's Treats mini on the way out.

S

2018–2021

Thirty-Three

MORE MYSELF

I'm not a California girl. But LA continued to capture Kyle's and my interest. We started spending long weekend days popping into open houses "for fun," until we walked into a house, frozen in time in 1986, and fell in love with the view.

"I don't even care what the house looks like," I said, admiring the ocean and cityscape. "We have to live here."

Before one trip, I'd been frantically dealing with the onslaught of the September mom rush: forms, sign-ups, new events, new teachers, new everything. I had so many emails and tasks to do for the kids that I barely had time to be with them. And being with them was why I'd "stayed home." Not to be a glorified assistant, arranging and reconfirming playdates, coordinating after-school drop-offs and activities, managing teacher requests, and sending in medical claim forms. To actually *be* with the kids!

"Mama, come play 'floor is lava,'" my daughter would ask as I sat hunched forward at my desk.

"Hold on, honey," I'd say. "I have a few more emails to do. But they're all about you!"

It was no consolation.

Plus I had limited time anyway, as the next custody drop-off always loomed ahead. I was getting fed up.

The last straw?

"Hi, parents!" the preschool teacher wrote. "Reminder! We're collecting supplies for our next craft project and need all of you to please bring in at least four cardboard toilet paper rolls tomorrow!"

Seriously? Now I would have to go around the house unspooling reams of toilet paper so I didn't disappoint the teachers? I didn't want to do that. I wanted to sit on the floor and help build Legos! I wanted to take the kids out for frozen yogurt at Sixteen Handles. Read them some of their favorite books, like Mo Willems's Elephant & Piggie series, with us all acting out different characters, or Oliver Jeffers's *How to Catch a Star*. Not go on an adult scavenger hunt.

I'd. Had. Enough.

No more. I would reclaim my time with my kids and revolt.

That night, after another tearful doorstep goodbye to the kids when they went to their dad's, Kyle and I went straight to the airport to head to LA. On the quiet, humming plane, encased in the metal security of the giant cross-country machine, I flipped open my laptop and wrote an essay I called "A Mother's Right to Sanity."

I was putting my foot down on behalf of all other mothers. I couldn't be the only one who was chronically overwhelmed by what the demands of motherhood had morphed into over the years. I was sure this wasn't what my mom had to do between running to her own nonprofit board meetings, going to Gilda's aerobics classes, and taking my brother and me to playdates, occasionally driving us to a friend's house all the way on the west side.

I typed and vented, sipping water from the plastic cup on my tray table, until all my frustrations were out. My demand: let us moms just be moms!

When we got to the hotel, I climbed into bed, ensconced myself in fluffy hotel bedding, and uploaded the piece to HuffPost. When I woke up in the morning, HuffPost had moved it from the contributor platform, which allowed any writer to post anything, to its front page.

"Honey!" I said, scanning the site. "Look! They liked that essay!"

Kyle rolled over and peeked at the screen.

"Nice, love!"

I had 10,000 views.

By the end of the day, 65,000 people had read it. I hoped they were other moms, cheering me on as I stood up for our collective well-being. Yes, these were high-class "woe is me" problems, but as a society, we were leaning heavily on mothers to do too much. I had to speak up.

I read *Bad Mother: A Chronicle of Maternal Crimes, Minor Calamities, and Occasional Moments of Grace* by Ayelet Waldman, *Free-Range Kids* by Lenore Skenazy, *Motherhood Comes Naturally (and Other Vicious Lies)* by Jill Smokler, *Does This Volvo Make My Butt Look Big? Thoughts for Moms and Other Tired People* by Annabel Monaghan, *I Just Want to Pee Alone* by Jen Mann and other mom bloggers, *The Fifth Trimester* by Lauren Smith Brody, and all of Stefanie Wilder-Taylor's books.

I knew what I was doing was reaching people and helping them feel less alone.

So I kept doing it.

I wrote essays on topics like why I refused to keep being my kids' personal assistant (even though I still made all the playdate arrangements), or why we moms should decide collectively to lose weight later and take the pressure off ourselves now. I wrote about how we could reclaim sleep, why I cried on the bathroom floor even though I knew how lucky I was, and how we should all save time by not getting our nails done. I basically shouted from the HuffPost, ScaryMommy, MommyNearest, and Today Show Parenting Team pages that mothers couldn't do it all anymore. We just couldn't. It was too much. We needed a break—and we needed to be the ones to fight for it.

Several months later, before bed, I'd just finished reading Kyle one of my essays, which I did whenever I wrote anything; he always had great suggestions.

"Honey, you should really take all your parenting essays and make them into a book."

"Ugh," I said, waving my hands dismissively at the idea. "Moms don't have time to read books!"

Then I giggled.

"Oh, that's perfect," I said. "That'll be the name of it!"

Thirty-Four

THE REJECTION THAT CHANGED MY LIFE

I mean, I could really do a better job at this.

I was sitting on a wooden pew at my kids' school for the weekly Friday assembly to which all parents and lower schoolers were invited. Life had resumed that fall like it had every other crazy year before it. With Kyle's and my new apartment decorated, our lives blended, our wedding done, I finally had the time and mental energy to focus on something new.

Teachers, special guests, and students would perform for thirty minutes, always centered on a certain theme. That year's theme? Voice.

As I watched an English teacher read a children's book to the zoned-out audience, I started brainstorming other assembly ideas.

In my head, I started writing a speech to present. As a shy child, I'd found my voice through writing. Perhaps I could share my experience and help the other shy kids sitting out there?

Back home afterward, I banged out the speech I would make. I made jokes, gave tips, added some pictures as visual aids, and made it fun and relatable to lower schoolers. I sent it off to the school, suggesting I lead the assembly one morning. Why not?

They said yes.

Two months later, I was the one standing behind the lectern, in front of a giant screen, the pictures I'd selected rotating through. One was a photo of the group I was in for our required freshman-year trip to Frost Valley, a time when I literally couldn't speak and one mean girl had made fun of me.

"See my group?" I said to the kids, pointing at the picture. "I wasn't even in the picture! Look all the way on the right where that blur is. Those were my shorts!"

Everyone laughed.

In the speech, I made a joke about not having an agent and said, "If anyone knows a good one, please send them my way."

On my way out of the school building, a mom I didn't know with curly brown hair and an infectious smile ran over to me.

"Hi! I'm Sarah. Loved your speech. You don't really need an agent, do you?"

"I do!"

I'd written a proposal for the book of parenting essays Kyle had suggested I write: *Moms Don't Have Time to Read Books*.

"Let's get coffee. I'm a middle grade novelist. I have so many ideas for you."

It was Sarah Mlynowski, the bestselling author of the Whatever After series and coauthor of the Upside-Down Magic series, which my kids loved.

A week later, we were sitting at a tiny coffee shop near school as she flipped through my book proposal.

"I'll send this to my agent," she said, scanning it. "But I don't know. I just don't think this is the right project for you. This might sound weird, but I have a gift of knowing what people should do next. I'm not sure about you, but it'll come to me."

"Okay," I said, skeptical. I mean, I'd just met her.

"But yeah, I've actually gotten some other advice recently that essay collections don't sell, especially about motherhood. And I don't have a 'platform.'" It was 2018, and I wasn't even on social media.

Meanwhile, I'd met a literary agent named Rachel Horowitz, who soon ended up representing me. I'd just gotten on Instagram, Facebook, and Twitter and noticed that she was following me. At a local pottery place, the Craft Studio, with the kids, I'd direct messaged her, saying, "Hi! You're my fifth follower! Just wondering how you even heard about me?"

Rachel responded that she was also a parent at my kids' school and had recognized my name. After finding me, she had done a deep dive into the essays on my website. Would I have time to talk?

Um, yes.

I wrote back, "How about now?"

I left my kids painting overpriced ceramic cats and called her from the street.

"So do you have a book in you?" she asked.

"Funny you should say that. I have a proposal for a book of parenting essays."

She sighed.

"Well, essays don't really sell, especially about parenting. Plus you have no platform."

"I've been publishing essays since I was fourteen years old."

"Yeah, but that doesn't help. You hardly have any followers."

"I mean, I literally just signed up for all of my accounts."

"And you're not famous or anything. I don't think you'll be able to sell it."

"Do you want to even read it?"

"Sure, send it over. But do you have any other ideas?"

A few weeks later, we met for coffee at Shakespeare & Co. bookstore on Lexington Avenue.

"I read your proposal," she said. "Again, it just won't sell. I'm sorry. It's the whole essay category. Do you have any other ideas?"

"Well," I said, "what I really want to do is write a memoir called *40 Love* about falling in love again at age forty with my tennis pro. But I can't."

"Why? That sounds fantastic."

"I just can't. There's too much private stuff."

"I think you should write that book and see where it goes."

"Maybe. We'll see. Maybe I'll try it."

Back at coffee with Sarah Mlynowski, she was saying the same thing.

"I'll think of something else," she said, "and I'll introduce you to my agent, just in case. We'll figure this out."

Her agent passed on representing me. But Sarah changed my life.

———

As I rushed out of the crowded school lobby after drop-off the next week, Sarah was rushing in.

"A podcast!" she called out as she passed by me, throngs of students and parents surrounding us.

"What?"

"A podcast! You should start a podcast!"

"What's a podcast?"

Back at home, I sat on the couch in my new office next to Kyle, staring at my phone.

"I don't even see a button for podcasts on here, do you?"

It was early 2018. Podcasts were already booming, but I had missed the trend. Thanks to Google, we downloaded the app and then started listening to a few episodes of popular shows.

What would I even do a podcast *about*?

I researched how to start a podcast and then put the idea out of my head. Meanwhile I was using my new Facebook account to send around articles I found or essays I liked. Usually, I'd just rip articles out of the actual, physical paper or magazines and mail them to friends. Now I could forward articles to all my "friends" instantly. What if I read the articles as a podcast for the moms who didn't even have time to read what I sent? And I could read parts of books I loved!

Perhaps if my mom friends listened to me read while they did other things, they could squeeze in books and articles. I'd always found so much value and comfort in reading other people's personal essays. I was sure others would, too. We didn't have time to get together for coffee like we used to, but surely we could all listen to the same podcast and feel that same level of connection?

I also figured I could read my *own* essays. Despite some of them reaching large audiences, I always felt frustrated sitting at my desk, watching the numbers on Medium languish and knowing that there were moms out there who were also feeling terrible about their bodies or struggling to remember their kids' teachers' names or enduring something else we all felt and perhaps didn't say. But I wasn't able to reach them. How could I get my *own* content out there?

While unpacking my tote bag of books in our hotel room at La Quinta in Palm Springs, where Kyle and I were staying to watch the Indian Wells tennis tournament, I gasped.

"Honey!" I ran over to Kyle. "I know what to do for my podcast! I'll use that name from the book of essays, *Moms Don't Have Time to Read Books*, and read articles, books, and my own articles to help moms who are too busy to even read them!"

"Love it! That's a great idea!"

I headed back to my huge TBR (to be read) stack with a sense of purpose. *You Are a Badass* by Jen Sincero, *The Glass Castle* by Jeannette Walls, *The Nightingale* by Kristin Hannah, *My Name Is Lucy Barton* by Elizabeth Strout, and *Shoe Dog* by Phil Knight.

I commissioned a logo on 99designs and googled "how to start a podcast from your phone." I signed up for Podbean because that claimed to be the easiest platform. I listened to a few more podcasts, enlisted my first sponsor, Chloe's Treats, and got ready to record. Why not? I wouldn't tell anyone at first. I'd just do it.

In the meantime, I started writing *40 Love*. At least I'd have the book for myself, I rationalized. Maybe I'd forget some of the details of my crazy years if I didn't write about them soon.

I wrote whenever I could: waiting in doctors' offices, on the floor in the mornings while the kids played, in bed during long stretches on those quiet weekends without the kids, on all of our many flights. Whenever Kyle and I would travel, especially to LA, I'd revel in the time to pound out my story. Kyle joked at the end that I had written almost the entire thing in the sky.

Then I decided to turn it into a novel with similar themes, but completely different characters and plot. I rewrote it a third time, basing it in LA and changing just about everything except the feelings. On one flight from Athens to New York after Kyle and I had spent a week relaxing on Mykonos (woe is me, I know), I started it yet again. I spent eleven hours straight typing and landed with a literary novella in hand—and carpal tunnel syndrome.

Meanwhile, I'd realized my podcast content plan was illegal. I couldn't just read from copyrighted articles and books. Perhaps I could interview the authors directly?

I wasn't sure how to pull that off; I knew only about three authors. But I could try. If worse came to worst, I could just read my own articles and send the episodes to friends.

I hadn't been on social media until launching the Nene's Treats Instagram account a few months earlier, so I didn't know that authors had blasted onto the scene themselves via Instagram, Twitter, and Facebook. Anyone could follow an author and see what they had for breakfast, what their dog looked like, and even where they were writing.

Author John Kenney, who wrote *Love Poems for Married People*, recently posted a picture of his book in progress—the pages taped to the wall stretched up to the molding. I simply commented, "Good thing you're so tall. My book would have to be half as long!" The inside look into authors' lives came as a complete shock to me. How amazing! Perhaps I could access them directly?

For my first podcast episode, I went into my bedroom and read my article "A Mother's Right to Sanity" into my phone. Then I googled equipment and bought a Blue Yeti microphone. I taught myself how to use GarageBand to record.

My friend and former editor Lea Carpenter was my first guest. Before our interview—and before my first two hundred or so episodes—I would type out detailed questions ahead of time, including quotes from the book, and send them along first so the guests wouldn't be surprised. As Lea and I spoke, I learned new things about her, despite having known her well for the previous seventeen years. And I loved it. I just loved it! I loved the intimacy of the interview setting, the absence of small talk, the deep conversations, and the complete focus. Time stopped. All I cared about was our chat. I was hooked. But how could I find more authors?

As luck would have it, Kyle's former tennis colleague Murphy Jensen, French Open doubles champion, had just sat next to Andre Agassi on a flight. I overheard him telling Kyle about it on FaceTime and I walked over and said, "Murphy! Do you think there's any chance in the world Andre Agassi would come on my podcast? *Open* was one of my favorite books of all time."

"Well, it doesn't hurt to ask!"

Andre miraculously said yes.

I still have his text messages in my phone. Heart emojis!

Since Andre was remote, I had to teach myself how to interview using Skype and then turn the files into MP3s. This was before the Zoom era. I was so nervous, my hands were literally shaking.

During the interview, I sat at my desk and asked Andre about his book, his life, his new position as Novak Djokovic's coach, and his new company. I sweat so much I had to change clothes afterward. When we finished, I raced downstairs to Kyle and the kids, who were watching TV.

"I did it!" I said, bursting into the room. "It was so cool!"

Once I released Lea's and Andre's episodes, my podcast was off and running. Through word of mouth and my own outreach, more authors agreed to come on. Delia Owens was an early guest. Dani Shapiro, one of my favorite authors, agreed to come on after I sat with her at the New York Public Library's Library Lunch. As Dani chatted with me at my desk before *Inheritance* even came out, I couldn't believe it. I had dragged Kyle to public events with Dani in LA at Diesel bookstore and the Hotel Bel-Air, and back in New York at The Corner Bookstore on Madison Avenue. Now here she was, in my home office, suggesting I start a salon series. She even offered to do the first event. I couldn't believe it. Of course I said yes.

I ended up organizing a panel discussion with Dani and Piper Weiss, author of *You All Grow Up and Leave Me*, with a book fair in my dining room. I sold all the books I'd covered on the podcast, invited all the authors, and sold the books through BookHampton, a bookstore in East Hampton. In my three book fairs over two years, I sold over $20,000 worth of books for that independent bookstore and hosted hundreds of authors.

Publicists started pitching author clients. I grew more ambitious in my asks. In fact, I tried for years to get Anna Quindlen on my show and kept getting turned down until Jean Hanff Korelitz, bestselling author of *The Plot*, and friend from my author salon series, introduced us. Now we email frequently. Anna not only came on the podcast, but she even participated in Zibby's Virtual Book Club, which I started during the pandemic.

I just kept asking. Reading. Preparing. Interviewing. It was like meeting famous rock stars every day. Many authors came over to do the recording in person. I hosted events where I'd connect authors like Liz Astrof, *Don't Wait Up: Confessions of a Stay-at-Work Mom*, and Helen Ellis, *Southern Lady Code*, with John Kenney, *Love Poems for People with Children*. Or Abby Maslin, *Love You Hard*, and Allison Pataki, *Beauty in the Broken Places*, with Lori Gottlieb, *Maybe You Should Talk to Someone*. Soon authors like Jennifer Weiner and Mitch Albom would pop in when they were in town for big media hits. I couldn't believe it. I'd make them a cup of coffee in my kitchen and then head upstairs to record.

Many authors I interviewed cried, like *Lost* star Evangeline Lilly, *The Squickerwonkers*; Mitch Albom about his new book, *Finding Chika*; and Teresa Sorkin, *The Woman in the Park*. Others, like Sarah McColl, *Joy Enough*, arrived super nervous for their first book interview ever. I spoke to old friends like Stacey's and my friend Rebecca, now professionally known as Rebecca Schrag Hershberg, PhD, who wrote *The Tantrum Survival Guide*, and Lauren Braun Costello, coauthor with Russell Reich of *Notes on Cooking*. Claire Bidwell Smith, *The Rules of Inheritance*, brought her baby to our interview in LA. We took turns bouncing him as we spoke. Authors invited me to moderate their launch events.

Jamie Brenner, who wrote *Drawing Home*, asked me to interview her at her Barnes & Noble launch event on the Upper East Side. Of course! I brought Kyle, the four kids, my mom, and Tenzin to watch. I'd never been more excited about anything. Finally, I would be the one onstage instead of in the audience! Barnes & Noble! By the time the pandemic hit, I'd done in-person events at Shakespeare & Co. (with Rochelle Weinstein and Lisa Barr), McNally Jackson, BookHampton, two Barnes & Nobles in Manhattan (one with Nicola Harrison), The Center for Fiction, Berry & Co. (with Courtney Maum), Rizzoli Bookstore, Temple Emanu-El's Streicker Center, and many other locations, including dozens of my own salons.

———

A year into hosting the podcast, the salon events, and the book fairs, I realized that James Frey, author of *A Million Little Pieces*, would be in LA doing an event at Book Soup for his new novel, *Katerina*, on a weekend when Kyle and I were scheduled to be there. Kyle had taught James and his family tennis. When I reached out to his publicist to request an interview, I mentioned Kyle's connection. The publicist wrote back: "Would you be willing to meet James in his hotel the morning after the event for an interview?" Yes! Yes, I would. Ever since that moment at my mom's house when we watched Oprah together, I'd felt like I needed to hear what had happened. It had felt personal.

Kyle and I drove down Sunset Boulevard along the windy, palm tree–lined road from the Pacific Palisades to West Hollywood to attend the event that night. I wanted to be as prepared as possible for my interview.

At Book Soup, James read a passage from *Katerina* and then answered questions. Every sentence he uttered was peppered liberally with the words "fuck" or "asshole."

The next morning, Kyle and I walked into the marble lobby of the London hotel. I'd recently interviewed Min Jin Lee to discuss *Pachinko* in the tiny business center by the front door of the Peninsula hotel and had set up my microphone—and desktop!—in a random conference room at the Essex House hotel to record my session with Senator Kirsten Gillibrand, so I knew I could do my interview anywhere.

James was late. Very late. I emailed his publicist and she eventually told me he'd overslept but would be down soon to meet us. Kyle and I browsed the gift shop in the lobby. I picked up a retro brown-and-white desk placard name sign that said something about motherfuckers that I thought he'd find funny. (He did.)

Eventually, James showed up in his pajama pants, looking disoriented and needing coffee, which we got at the hotel bar. Would we mind coming upstairs to do the interview?

The three of us rode up quietly in the mirrored elevator. I caught sight of my reflection and almost started laughing. I mean, really. What was I doing there?

James's bed was unmade and clothes were scattered everywhere, the shades drawn. He casually swiped everything off the one desk by the window, chomping on Nicorette gum.

"This okay?"

"It's great."

I stepped over his laundry.

"I'll make it work."

Once I started recording, James came alive, telling stories, opining on content development and creativity, discussing writing and reading. I asked him about his new book, the difference between fiction and memoir, and then went for it.

I dove right into the whole Oprah issue: when she had him admit that his memoir wasn't all truth. I asked him what it had been like, how he had felt in that moment, how he felt about it now. He confessed how embarrassed he'd been, how it was the worst day of his life.

Until our conversation, I hadn't realized *Katerina* had been mostly true.

"Well, if I call it a memoir, I get in trouble. So I call it fiction," he said.

Despite all the controversy, I still think *A Million Little Pieces* is one of the best books ever written. And that James Frey has some mother-fucking talent.

Thirty-Five

MODERN MADNESS

My daughter's teacher was working her magic with the white-board. The kindergarten classroom was filled with dads in suits and moms dressed up for Parents' Night, all contorted to fit into tiny wooden chairs designed for kids who were at most four feet tall. As I tried to catch my breath, I pondered whether I was the only one who missed blackboards and erasers, the swirl of chalk in the air, the faint remnants of the last lesson peeking out from under the smudges.

I had just sprinted across Central Park. My daughter had made me promise not to miss the video of her puppet show and the accompanying project that was to be showcased that evening.

And it was the week of the UN General Assembly, an international conference that descends on Manhattan each fall at the worst possible time, stranding families, halting traffic, ruining plans, and generally causing complete mayhem in an already packed metropolis.

I was wearing a long skirt and striped sweater with Vans and had actually dried my hair for this social event. I'd left my four kids at home just before our family dinner, which I hated to miss, and I gave myself an hour to spare for the twelve-minute drive. But my Uber had progressed only an inch at a time for the first thirty minutes. I kept looking at my watch. The time ticked by as I pinged away on my cell phone, hoping the traffic would let up.

Then, it was time. Either I had to hop out of the car and run the rest of the way or I'd miss the puppet presentation. So I grabbed my purse, swung open the car door on Eighty-Fifth and Fifth, slammed it shut, and started running. I didn't have time to find the closest scenic entrance to Central Park. I ran right into the transverse designed exclusively for cars, with only a slim sidewalk for the single-lane corridor that connects the east and west sides of Manhattan.

I could do this! If I just ran a little faster, I could do it. Or maybe I could find a cab now that I'd passed the barricade? I tiptoed to the center of the road to peer around the bend and a cab zoomed around and almost hit me, blaring its horn as I jumped back onto the curb.

"Oh my Lord," I thought. "How perfect would this be? *Mom dies sprinting across the park for Parents' Night.*"

I seemed to have forgotten that I was in my forties and hadn't been working out. At all. I couldn't just jump up and run a couple of miles without any preparation—and with Olympic speed. What was I thinking!? The fumes from the stream of cars filtered into my hair like cheap dry shampoo. And I was sweating. A lot. So much for the outfit. And the hair.

It was approaching 6:00 p.m. As I caught sight of Central Park West, I slowed down to a walk. I still had several blocks to go and I was hurting.

But the puppets! What if I missed it? I couldn't show up at home and admit defeat. So I took a deep breath and started running again. I raced down the paved stones lining the park and across town to the school entrance. I passed a few parents slowly strolling down the block and leaped past the Lower School principal, a lovely blonde woman waiting at the front door to shake all of our hands like she did for our kids each day.

As I quickly shook her hand, she said, "Slow down! Nothing has started yet!"

I was huffing and puffing but nodded, giving her a thumbs-up, as I started climbing the stairs to my daughter's classroom. This was my third kid to start at this school, plus I'd gone there for high school, so I knew the building like the back of my hand. The school staircase? I could do it in my sleep.

A few more steps and I threw open the door. The teacher had just started welcoming the parents.

Squeezing through all the other parents who greeted me with a smile or a surprised look as I pressed my sweaty body between them to get to the closest chair, I could feel that I was making a commotion. The conversation stopped as everyone turned to look at me.

"Sorry, I just ran across the park!"

"Wow!" the teacher said. "That's dedication."

As soon as I sat down, a hippie-dippie mom friend leaned forward and, in a low, sultry voice, slowly said, "I can't believe you just did that for your third child. I wouldn't even have showed up."

Meanwhile, other parents kept entering late, not at all frazzled, just holding up their hands and saying, "Sorry, UN traffic." Why hadn't I been able to do that?

A few minutes later, I noticed that I couldn't get my breathing back to normal. I coughed. Again. And again. I kept clearing my throat, trying not to be disruptive. And yet, I couldn't breathe. The hippie mom tapped me on the shoulder with her Poland Spring bottle, wordless, offering it up.

"Thank you!" I mouthed.

I tried to focus on the presentation: the field trips coming up, the goals for kindergarten, the curriculum in science and gym. But did I even need to listen? I knew all of this. My two older kids had already done it. I could actually teach this seminar.

The water didn't help. I decided to squeeze back out and try the old-fashioned water fountain, drinking what my kids call "sink water." I doubled over to drink from the small sink and felt like Alice in

Wonderland. At five feet two inches, I wasn't used to anything being too short for me.

Okay, that would probably do the trick.

Back in my seat, waiting for the puppet show video, I began to panic. Something was wrong. My twins both had food allergies, and once or twice I'd broken out in hives after a run. "Am I seriously having an allergic reaction right now?" I thought. "Was it something in the transverse? Where is the nearest EpiPen?"

I wondered if the school nurse was on duty for Parents' Night. Probably not. And with UN week, I couldn't just hop in a cab and get to the hospital. With all the traffic, I probably wouldn't make it, even if I called an ambulance. Is this it? For the second time that hour, I thought about the irony of dying right then. *Mom dies at Parents' Night; no EpiPen on hand for parents!* A piece on allergies would follow.

But look! There was the puppet movie! I coughed and sputtered like an old Buick as I watched the two-second clip of my daughter on the screen, proudly showing off her creation. It made me smile. I'd done it.

Somehow, by the end of the presentation, I'd slowed my breathing enough to realize I wasn't going to die that evening, although it would take another couple of hours to feel completely fine again. I stood up, my knees creaking, and chitchatted with the other parents as we all walked back downstairs. I ducked out before the cocktail hour so I could deal with all the kids at home.

Before I went to bed that night, I got a mass email from the teacher.

"For those of you who may have missed it, here's the video of your child's puppet performance!"

Are you kidding me?! I could've skipped the entire event!

The next day, I wrote an essay about my ridiculousness and sent it around to the parents in the class as a mea culpa. One mom stopped me at drop-off as we helped our little ones hang up their tiny coats side by side.

"I loved your essay," she said, smiling at me. "I thought I was the only one who felt like that last night. I was freaking out about the traffic. Seriously, why is UN week in New York!?"

We laughed.

"I'm so glad it helped," I said.

Per usual, in my haste to go at superspeed, I risked missing the plot.

As it turned out, that mom worked at Gersh, a talent agency, and introduced me to Joe Veltre, a literary agent who sat in the office next to hers. He invited me into the office for a meeting and took me on as his client. Finally, I had an agent again! My new mantra: everything happens as it's supposed to. Also: don't miss the plot.

Thirty-Six

ALL THIS TIME

When the pandemic hit, I moved out to Water Mill with Kyle and the kids. We invited Susan and Nene to join us, but they demurred; they had two dogs and didn't want to impose. They also thought it would be safer to stay where they were in North Carolina; at the time, New York was the epicenter of the virus in the United States. The next morning on the trampoline, I came up with the idea to host an hour-long Instagram Live show five days a week, with four to five authors each "show," which I did for several months.

I had to do *something* to help all the authors with books coming out during the lockdown. All that hard work! I also released several original personal essays each week by authors from the podcast, which, after the pandemic, I turned into my first anthology, *Moms Don't Have Time To: A Quarantine Anthology*. It included over sixty essays by authors from the podcast and was published by Skyhorse Publishing. All proceeds went to Covid-19 research. Ironically, I found out I had Covid a few days before that book came out (my "pub day"). I did all press events from bed with terrible vertigo. That anthology led to a second anthology with over fifty essays called *Moms Don't Have Time to Have Kids*, which became an Amazon bestseller. During the pandemic, I also started a virtual book club, which met every week (and now meets monthly). I helped as much as I could.

The authors got even more exciting. Alicia Keys, *More Myself*. Lena Dunham, *Not That Kind of Girl*. Chelsea Clinton, *She Persisted*. Jill Biden, *Where the Light Enters*, before she became the First Lady. Cheryl Strayed, *Wild*. Natalie Portman, *Natalie Portman's Fables*. Jenna Bush Hager, *Everything Beautiful in Its Time*.

Everything was growing. My downloads. My Instagram followers. I started writing a regular column for *Good Morning America*, picking the best books of the month. I went on the news regularly to suggest titles. I wrote for the *Washington Post*. I signed a two-book deal with Flamingo, a division of Penguin Random House, for a children's book character named Princess Charming. Joe Veltre and I had sold four books together. It was insane. I couldn't believe how quickly things were taking off.

The previous summer, I'd met with a savvy venture capitalist, Maxine Kozler, who said I had to put myself out there to really grow my brand. Personal enhancement or fame was never a goal of mine, but I remember that meeting, sitting under an umbrella by a pool in LA overlooking the city and making the conscious choice that I would do it. I would let myself become the spokeswoman of the brand. I'd put myself out there in order to grow my platform and help more authors and readers.

———

The more authors I spoke to on the podcast, the more I realized that being a writer was a trait shared by some of the most amazing people on the planet. That need to tell a story, to share, to help others, to use words as memories, as tools to evoke emotions, reflected a lot about the person, even more than the content they wrote. They were my people. (My other theory is that a vast majority of authors have anxiety disorders, like me.)

I'd always considered myself a writer. Not a successful one, of course, and not necessarily a published one, but deep in my heart, I've always known that's who I am. (When I was a stay-at-home mom, I joked that I should call myself a nonpracticing writer.) After speaking to hundreds of authors, I realized that was usually the case for them, too. Life events conspired to strip that label away from most people, whether through failure, lack of time, or lack of resources. But nothing could rob the soul of that spiritual instinct and desire to share the contents of one's mind with someone else. Fiction writers, I thought, were particularly amazing—not just wondering about the lives of the strangers at the next restaurant table, but imagining and crafting full-on narratives about them.

Sometimes now I fantasize about writing a novel in which everyone's characters meet and mingle. I've gotten to know so many fictitious characters that I could craft a novel around them. I want to introduce the main character in Elyssa Friedland's *Last Summer at the Golden Hotel* to the main character in Lauren Weisberger's *Where the Grass Is Green and the Girls Are Pretty*. Those two women should be friends! Like an episode of *All in the Family* when the Jeffersons would pop over, I'd love to see characters intermix between books.

I would read a book from start to finish in a single morning. Skimming or speed-reading still gave me the hit of dopamine I extracted from reading. It reset my emotions and wiped the slate clean. I prepped and underlined and dog-eared pages and researched authors.

While I homeschooled my four kids, did a zillion loads of laundry, interviewed authors, and read, I slowly started seeing how I could change the book world.

Thirty-Seven

Living Out Loud

Tragedy struck.

Kyle's amazing mom, Susan, and his grandmother Nene both died of Covid six weeks apart in the summer of 2020. Nene went to the hospital for a preexisting condition and caught Covid, bringing it home and giving it to Susan. Susan stuffed her hazmat suit with ice packs to bring down her fever when saying goodbye to her mom in the Covid unit. The day after Nene passed away, Susan was admitted. Kyle, Stefanie, and I were in charge of her care, speaking to doctors and nurses every three hours for weeks on end. Susan suffered. She had a protracted, ugly, brutal death after a six-week struggle in three hospitals on ventilators and on an ECMO machine. By the time she passed away, she had suffered multiple strokes and couldn't move the right side of her body. Covid ravaged her lungs so swiftly and viciously that doctors looking at her chest X-rays were shocked she didn't have any prior health issues.

Susan was all alone except for the last couple of days, when Kyle and Stefanie were allowed to say goodbye. I drove them and waited in the car downstairs, ferrying them to and from the ICU in those final days, taking care of the dogs in a small hotel suite at Duke. It was horrific. When the doctors called to tell us she was gone, the dogs, always perfectly behaved, attacked each other as Stefanie doubled over and wailed. I'll never forget that moment and that guttural, animal sound.

Kyle will never be the same. None of us will. Undiagnosed PTSD settled into our home like low-lying fog on a morning soccer field. We adopted Nya, Susan's black lab, and Stefanie took Luna. Nya has been my true emotional support animal, curling into the bend in my knees and sleeping snuggled next to me every night since that horrific evening at Duke. Kyle's dad and Stefanie both moved to New York so they could all be closer. Stefanie now runs Nene's Treats herself, still selling the delicious crumb cakes direct to customers on Goldbelly.com. (Subtle hint: buy one!)

Gagy died from natural causes at age ninety-seven. Another sorrow I grieved intensely without the support of family and friends, another virtual funeral. Unlike the shiva in Dayton for Papa Kal, I couldn't even go to Gagy's apartment to say goodbye. The clock that Papa Kal carved by hand, the one that chimed in their foyer all these years, is now in the corner of our master bedroom in New York. The time has stopped.

Through it all, I turned to books. *Widowish* by Melissa Gould. Sara Evans, *Born to Fly*. Nora McInerny, *No Happy Endings*. Leslie Gray Streeter's *Black Widow*. Stephanie Thornton Plymale's *American Daughter*. Kara Goldin's *Undaunted*. Brit Bennett, *The Vanishing Half*. I read and read and read. Through Zoom school. Through Zoom life. Through complete isolation with just us and the kids for months on end. I read. I listened to audiobooks. I launched *Moms Don't Have Time to Write* on Medium to publish other people's personal essays, now led by Jordan Blumetti and Emily Sharp. I started Moms Don't Have Time to Grieve, helmed by Sherri Puzey. I started a podcast and Instagram community called Moms Don't Have Time to Lose Weight. I got jolts of life, vitality, creativity, and purpose from every story. And all that kept me going so I could keep everyone else afloat.

People always ask me how I do it. Do I have a clone? How could I possibly fit it all in? I just do. I do it because the more I do it, the more energy I have. Because I love it. It's my life's purpose, what author Eve Rodsky would identify as my "unicorn space." It's how I get through the moments that seem insurmountable. Sometimes I actually have to force myself to do *less*; moderation has always been a challenge for me.

Luckily, I'm fast. I do everything at superspeed, even typing. When something needs to get done, I do it right away. And the more I do it all, the faster I get, even the speed at which I read. I used to think reading speed was a fixed trait. Now I know that the more you read, the faster you get at it. I bolt out of bed around 5:00 a.m. and keep going until my eyes shut around 10:30 p.m., a book usually open on my chest.

I'm finishing this book just after my forty-fifth birthday. Six years since Kyle sent me that song. Nineteen years since Papa Kal died. Twenty years since Stacey disappeared. For the twentieth anniversary of 9/11, I sat on my library couch with Rebecca and Allie, going through old newspaper clippings, eulogies, and photos of Stace. I've met hundreds of new people, found my tribe, and rediscovered who I really am.

Ultimately, I've found my purpose on earth, something worth dying at my desk for. I've raised four amazing, special kids who continue to surprise, delight, and teach me. I've helped people I know and people I've never met who listen to my podcast, which has been downloaded millions of times. I've become a top writer on Medium and am no longer bashing my head against the wall, knowing my essays could be helping more people. Thousands of dedicated, loyal followers on social media really feel like they know me. Because they do, in a way. I just don't know them . . . yet.

I've gone through the depths of grief, only to rise up again. And again. And again.

Because what choice did I have? My deep understanding that life is short and that I could be next propels me to follow my heart, stand up for what I believe in, and work hard to make a difference while I can. We get to do this only once. Time is ticking. Moms don't have time to waste.

Along the way, I've become a book messenger.

With all I've learned about the publishing industry from talking to almost a thousand authors—including, most recently, a live event with Hillary Rodham Clinton and bestselling author Louise Penny just two hours after their book *State of Terror* hit the *New York Times* bestseller list at number one—and from selling my own books, I decided to launch my own publishing company. I founded Zibby Books, with cofounder Leigh Newman, author of the memoir *Still Points North* and the short story collection *Nobody Gets Out Alive*. Jaunique Sealey (pen name: Jayne Allen), author of *Black Girls Must Die Exhausted*, heads up marketing, with Anne Messitte as our consulting publisher. Our whole team is amazing. I want to usher new stories into the world from start to finish, both memoirs and novels. Books that tell it like it is. I'm shaking up the industry paradigm and doing things differently. The media's reception of the publishing company has been fantastic: CNN, Katie Couric Media, *Forbes*, the *New York Post*, *Publishers Weekly*, Lit Hub, *Writer's Digest*, and more. I couldn't believe it.

Who knows where all of this will lead or what else I'll try? Ideas continue to percolate, including the launch of Zcast, my own podcast network powered by Acast. My car is now in drive, zooming down creativity lane with a full tank of gas. I don't want to miss a single stop. Sometimes I have to prevent myself from overdoing it and focus more on my own physical and mental health. The success itself is intoxicating.

Whatever happened to my novel *40 Love*, you might ask? I sent it out to five publishers the day the world shut down for the pandemic: March 12, 2020. But as Covid raged on, I found more and more flaws with it. Things I regretted. Parts I didn't like. It just wasn't right. Instead of sending it out to more publishers, I wanted the chance to tell my own story from the beginning and not have to hide the truth behind a novel.

And guess what?

I just did.

EPILOGUE

Want to hear my song?"

Over Labor Day weekend in 2021, Kyle and I sat side by side at dusk on the cushioned bench on the terrace of our home in Water Mill, where we'd spent most of the pandemic. His arm was casually draped around my shoulders as we peered out over the yard and the pool, the tennis court he designed—purple and green—just to the left of us.

Just inside, color-coded bookshelves were piled high with books for my podcast, including my own anthology from quarantine. An advance copy of my second anthology was en route to me via UPS. A printout of my upcoming children's book fluttered in the air-conditioning breeze on my desk. Back in Manhattan, my floor-to-ceiling office library of books had sat empty for the summer, stories swirling in the shadows, characters jumping back into books when the doors cracked open. The lights off.

The six of us—Kyle, me, and the four kids—were about to be separated for a few months. The TV, film, and music production company that Kyle had founded, Morning Moon, had its first feature film about to go into production. Kyle was going to spend three months in preproduction and then on the set of his movie, *Wildflower*, a project he'd discovered chatting with the eventual director while playing tennis in LA. He was right; it had all unfolded organically. Dan and Mike, the Dangermuffin duo who had practiced their performance in the basement on our wedding day, formed Morning Moon Music and now provide scores for ads and feature films. They've also released their own original music and have launched a new artist, Georgia VanNewkirk. They're doing the music for *Wildflower*.

My older son was going back to boarding school and the three other kids and I were headed to the city, where I knew I'd be insanely busy launching my publishing company, with multiple books coming out. And yet the September return didn't scare me anymore. I was ready for it.

Over the years, we had all become the best versions of ourselves, in large part thanks to Kyle.

My younger daughter cleared her throat. She was putting on an impromptu concert after dinner. A phenomenal singer and songwriter even at age eight, my daughter has always been filled with an innate sense of confidence, a Stacey and Paige level of self-assuredness. That first night in the hospital hearing Van Morrison when she was just a few hours old was a precursor to many more musical moments.

"Ready for the next song?" she asked.

"Yes, yes, let's hear it!" I said.

"Come on, rock star. You got this!" Kyle added.

She beamed at us.

Then, closing her eyes, her arms at her side, she took a deep breath and started singing.

This is my fight song.

ACKNOWLEDGMENTS

It takes a village.

Carmen Johnson from Little A took a risk on me when I sent out the proposal for this book, even after I sent her another note saying that I didn't have time to rewrite my sample chapter, but that I knew I could do better. Moms don't have time to write book proposals, I joked. Perhaps she laughed.

We brainstormed this entire book together, from the structure and scenes to the tone and tenor. It was a truly collaborative effort, exchanging Google Docs comments and Zooming about the best way to tell certain stories. I'm beyond lucky to have worked with her and truly can't say enough great things. This sounds like a reference letter. But I mean it!

Carmen, thank you. You've made my lifelong dream come true. I can't thank you enough.

Thanks also to my agent, Joe Veltre at Gersh, who didn't give up on me. He also spent hours listening to all of my ideas, trying to package them up in a way that would sell and make sense. He dealt with my eight million follow-ups and humored me when I assured him this one would sell on proposal. Without his confidence and willingness to keep sending things out there, I wouldn't have met Carmen, and these stories, these ghosts, would've stayed circling in my scalp or, perhaps, stayed pinned to my laptop, unread. I'm hoping my crazy little life story will help others out there. I mean, if I can do all of this, anyone can. So thanks, Joe. This is all you.

Thanks to all my early readers of this manuscript: my parents, my brother, Alyson Ein, Isabelle Krishana, Juad Masters, Genevieve McCormack, Tracey Cox, Cristina Alesci and Stephen Diamond, Anna Quindlen (!), Sean and Juliana McBride, and my team and the authors at Zibby Books. I intentionally didn't show this to any of my writer or editor friends for a long time because I was terrified they'd hate it and I'd have to change the whole thing. And I didn't have time!

Thanks to all the amazing people who blurbed this book: Arianna Huffington, Katie Couric, Kristin Hannah, Joanna Rakoff, Claire Bidwell Smith, Deborah Copaken, and Mitch Albom. I mean, really, what a list! I am humbled.

Thanks to Rachel Horowitz for encouraging me to write a memoir.

Thank you, Sarah Mlynowski, for telling me to start a podcast, something I never would've done and had never even considered, and for your friendship and mentorship ever since. Go Palisades!

Thanks to the hundreds of authors who have come on my podcast. You've opened up, told me your stories, connected, and brought your books to life.

Thanks to Acast for selling ads on the podcast, especially Sara Sopher and Grace Ross, and to Josh Lindgren at CAA for hooking that up.

Thanks to the authors of all the books mentioned in this book and the thousands of others I've read in my life that have moved me. Your characters live on, dancing on my bookshelves in the dark.

Thanks also to my friends, who I don't see enough. Actually, I don't even remember your names. Do you remember *me*?! Special shout-out to my "eke of inkling," Genevieve McCormack, and my Yale girls travel crew—Ann Jordan, Danielle Faris, Abby Johnston, Andrea Cheng, and Kate Lane—plus all of Stacey's many other Y98 friends, like Steve

Purdy, Victoria Lobis, Rachel Goulding, Sarah Saint-Amand, and so many more!

To my Group Six Breakfast Club girls: Carrie Quinn, Juad Masters, Lisa Frelinghuysen, Isabel Tonelli, Raja Clark, Whitney Topping, Pam Henes, Elizabeth Williams, Luleng Chua, Nancy Park, and Julie Richardson. We'll always miss our cheerleader, Paige Hardy.

Plus thanks to all my soul sisters, far and wide, even Nancy Badner, who was skeptical that this whole Kyle thing would work out! And to Rachel Young for being by my side during the HBS days.

And to Stacey's loved ones in the book: Allie Lewis, Bryan Koplin, Rebecca Schrag Hershberg, Abby Johnston (again), Abi Ross, and Sarah Irwin. There are no words. Who knew Stacey would bring us together in this way? Love always.

A special thank-you to my colleagues at Moms Don't Have Time To and Zibby Books: Leigh Newman, Anne Messitte, Jaunique Sealey, Chelsea Grogan, Jordan Blumetti, Emily Sharp, Sherri Puzey, Nina Vargas, Diana Tramontano, Tess Day, and Jeanne Emanuel (and to Chrystal Gray and Laura Rossi who have moved on, but we miss them!). Thanks to Kristin Lunghamer, my publicist at Little A.

Thanks to Margaret Anastas, Holly Hatam, Oliva Russo, and Elyse Marshall for bringing Princess Charming to life right before this book!

Thanks also to my podcast crew: sound editors Steve and Ryan at Textures Sound and Sara Grambusch at Bold Transcription. I couldn't do any of this without having an A-plus team like you all.

A special acknowledgment goes to Martha, John, and Laura Sanders; Tripp Hardy; and Didi Hockstader, who keep the spirits of Stacey, Paige, and Avery alive. To Adam's boys, Zachary, Nick, and Jay Henry; sisters, Betsey and Sara; and parents, Howard and Holly.

Thanks to all my exes—and their families.

Thanks to my many therapists along the way. You know who you are. And to Zoloft, which I couldn't live without.

Thanks to everyone out there who has followed along as I've built up my podcast into something bigger. It means so much to be part of a community together. Thanks to the Zibby Books ambassadors, my regulars from Zibby's Virtual Book Club, and my Instagram followers.

Thanks to my dad for everything, for all of this. Because of your hard work, Dad, I can help so many other people. It's a huge ripple effect. I'll never forget our lunch in the Spangler cafeteria when I realized that I'd have a far larger responsibility to the world than to myself. I try to honor that desire—and to be a leader who makes a difference in the world—daily.

Mom, thanks for fostering my love of reading and writing from day one. For not giving up on me. For all the homework help and for the exam elf. And for all the edits on this book.

To Howard for all the smiles and for being so amazing to Kyle. (Thanks, babe.)

Christine, thanks for making my dad so happy.

Teds, thanks for reading this and being so positive about it! Thanks for the title brainstorm (third try!), the reread, the feedback, and the Dodgers games. But more than that, thanks for being my copilot navigating our crazy lives together. And for all the tennis in LA. Thanks also to Ellen and the kids for all the fun, soccer games, and meals.

To all my aunts, uncles, and cousins, to my grandparents who are no longer here—thank you for including me in your clutches.

Thanks to everyone who helps me with my kids so I can stay sane and do all my work, like writing this book, especially Tenzin Palmo Patsatsang, who has been with me since 2006.

And speaking of kids, thanks to my four truly amazing children. You delight me daily. You inspire me. I'm so glad I haven't messed you up too much. Yet. This is short because what to say about the four souls that make my life worth living?? *I love you more.* ("My name is Zibby, I live in Zimbabwe, and I sell zebras!" "Frap day!" "Bud-Dee!")

To every editor who has ever published an essay or article of mine, thank you.

To every reader of anything I've written, especially this labor of love, thank you (yes, you!) for immersing yourself in my world and giving me the great honor of your time. It won't hurt my feelings if you don't finish reading this book. I'm just honored you read any of it (and, hopefully, bought it!). I know how busy we all are, so thank you.

Kyle. No words. You are insanely amazing. It was all worth it.

In loving memory of Nene (Marie Felice) and Susan Felice Owens. (Thank you with love to Stefanie, Bernard, and Miriam for stepping in and stepping up.)

Finally, to Fabio. If you hadn't gone on vacation, I never would've met Kyle.

This new life I'm leading really shouldn't be happening. It wasn't the plan. But then again, what is? As Kyle taught me, everything unfolds organically. Even memoirs.

(Note: I always feel compelled to write authors if I've loved their books. If you've even just *liked* my book, you can email me at zibby@bookendsmemoir.com. But if you don't have anything nice to say, don't say anything at all. Follow me on Instagram: @zibbyowens. I'll see you there!)

READING LIST

The following is a complete list of all the books referenced in *Bookends*. I hope you'll consider reading some of them. You can shop this list on my custom Bookshop.org and Amazon storefronts. Visit www.bookendsmemoir.com for links and a printable reading list.

The inclusion of an asterisk next to a title means there's an interview available with the author on my podcast *Moms Don't Have Time to Read Books*. Listen in!

FICTION

Albom, Mitch. *The Five People You Meet in Heaven**
Alcott, Louisa May. *Little Women*
Allen, Jayne. *Black Girls Must Die Exhausted: A Novel**
Allende, Isabel. *Daughter of Fortune*
Barr, Lisa. *The Unbreakables**
Bennett, Brit. *The Vanishing Half**
Bohjalian, Chris. *Midwives**
Brenner, Jamie. *Blush**; *Drawing Home**
Brown, Dan. *The Da Vinci Code*
Bushnell, Candace. *Sex and the City**
Camus, Albert. *L'étranger*

Carpenter, Lea. *Eleven Days**

Cleave, Chris. *Little Bee*

Clinton, Hillary Rodham and Louise Penny. *State of Terror**

Colwin, Laurie. *Family Happiness*

Conroy, Pat. *Beach Music*

Danler, Stephanie. *Sweetbitter**

Diamant, Anita. *The Red Tent**

Doerr, Anthony. *All the Light We Cannot See*

Donoghue, Emma. *Room*

Ephron, Nora. *Heartburn*

Esquivel, Laura. *Like Water for Chocolate: A Novel in Monthly Installments with Recipes, Romances, and Home Remedies*

Eugenides, Jeffrey. *The Virgin Suicides*

Fielding, Helen. *Bridget Jones's Diary*

Fossey, Brooke. *The Big Finish**

Fowler, Therese Anne. *Z: A Novel of Zelda Fitzgerald**

Freudenberger, Nell. *Lucky Girls: Stories**

Frey, James. *A Million Little Pieces**; *Bright Shiny Morning**; *Katerina**

Friedland, Elyssa. *Last Summer at the Golden Hotel**

Ganek, Danielle. *The Summer We Read Gatsby**

Giffin, Emily. *Something Borrowed**

Glass, Julia. *Three Junes*

Golden, Arthur. *Memoirs of a Geisha*

Guest, Judith. *Ordinary People*

Hannah, Kristin. *The Nightingale**

Harrison, Nicola. *Montauk**

Hemingway, Ernest. *A Farewell to Arms*

Hosseini, Khaled. *The Kite Runner*

Irving, John. *A Prayer for Owen Meany*

Johnson, Diane. *L'Affaire*

Kargman, Jill. *Momzillas**

Kinsella, Sophie. *Confessions of a Shopaholic**
Korelitz, Jean Hanff. *The Plot**
Krantz, Judith. *Princess Daisy; Scruples*
Lahiri, Jhumpa. *The Namesake*
Lamb, Wally. *I Know This Much Is True**
Larsson, Stieg. *The Girl with the Dragon Tattoo*
Lee, Min Jin. *Pachinko**
Martel, Yann. *Life of Pi*
Martin, Steve. *Shopgirl: A Novella*
Maum, Courtney. *Costalegre: A Novel Inspired by Peggy Guggenheim and Her Daughter, Pegeen**
McEwan, Ian. *Atonement; On Chesil Beach*
Mitchell, Margaret. *Gone with the Wind*
Moyes, Jojo. *Me Before You*
Newman, Leigh. *Nobody Gets Out Alive: Stories**
Ng, Celeste. *Little Fires Everywhere**
Norton, Ashley Prentice. *The Chocolate Money**
Owens, Delia. *Where the Crawdads Sing**
Peterson, Holly. *It's Hot in the Hamptons**
Plath, Sylvia. *The Bell Jar*
Proust, Marcel. *In Search of Lost Time*
Quindlen, Anna. *Black and Blue**
Reid, Taylor Jenkins. *Malibu Rising**
Salinger, J. D. *The Catcher in the Rye*
Sartre, Jean-Paul. *Huis clos, suivi de Les mouches*
Sebold, Alice. *The Lovely Bones*
Segal, Erich. *Love Story*
Smith, Zadie. *White Teeth*
Sorkin, Teresa and Tullan Holmqvist. *The Woman in the Park**
Sparks, Nicholas. *The Notebook**
Straub, Emma. *Modern Lovers**

Strout, Elizabeth. *My Name Is Lucy Barton*
Sweeney, Cynthia d'Aprix. *The Nest**
Tan, Amy. *The Bonesetter's Daughter*
Tartt, Donna. *The Goldfinch*
Towles, Amor. *Rules of Civility**
Tropper, Jonathan. *This Is Where I Leave You*
Verghese, Abraham. *Cutting for Stone*
Waller, Robert James. *The Bridges of Madison County*
Weiner, Jennifer. *Mrs. Everything**
Weisberger, Lauren. *The Devil Wears Prada**; *The Singles Game**; *Where the Grass Is Green and the Girls Are Pretty**
Weinstein, Rochelle B. *This Is Not How It Ends**
Wells, Rebecca. *Divine Secrets of the Ya-Ya Sisterhood*
Winston, Lolly. *Good Grief*
Wouk, Herman. *Marjorie Morningstar*

NONFICTION

Adams-Geller, Paige and Ashley Borden with Zibby Right. *Your Perfect Fit: What to Wear to Show Off Your Assets, What to Do to Tone Up Your Trouble Spots**
Astrof, Liz. *Don't Wait Up: Confessions of a Stay-at-Work Mom**
Auletta, Ken. *Greed and Glory on Wall Street: The Fall of the House of Lehman*
Bacal, Jessica. *The Rejection That Changed My Life: 25+ Powerful Women on Being Let Down, Turning It Around, and Burning It Up at Work**
Bourdain, Anthony and Laurie Woolever. *World Travel: An Irreverent Guide**
Bradley, James with Ron Powers. *Flags of Our Fathers*
Brody, Lauren Smith. *The Fifth Trimester: The Working Mom's Guide to Style, Sanity, and Big Success After Baby**

Brokaw, Tom. *The Greatest Generation*

Brown, Daniel James. *The Boys in the Boat: Nine Americans and Their Epic Quest for Gold at the 1936 Berlin Olympics**

Chapman, Gary. *The Five Love Languages: How to Express Heartfelt Commitment to Your Mate*

Chavarro, Jorge, Walter Willett, and Patrick Skerrett. *The Fertility Diet: Groundbreaking Research Reveals Natural Ways to Boost Ovulation and Improve Your Chances of Getting Pregnant*

Chupack, Cindy. *The Between Boyfriends Book: A Collection of Cautiously Hopeful Essays*

Clinton, Chelsea. *She Persisted: 13 American Women Who Changed the World**

Costello, Lauren Braun and Russell Reich. *Notes on Cooking: A Short Guide to an Essential Craft**

Cowley, Don. *Understanding Brands: By 10 People Who Do*

Diamant, Anita. *The New Jewish Wedding**

Duhigg, Charles. *The Power of Habit: Why We Do What We Do in Life and Business**

Ellis, Helen. *Southern Lady Code: Essays**

Ephron, Nora. *I Feel Bad About My Neck: And Other Thoughts on Being a Woman*

Fein, Ellen and Sherrie Schneider. *All the Rules: Time-Tested Secrets for Capturing the Heart of Mr. Right*

Freedman, Rory and Kim Barnouin. *Skinny Bitch: A No-Nonsense, Tough-Love Guide for Savvy Girls Who Want to Stop Eating Crap and Start Looking Fabulous!*

Gillibrand, Kirsten. *Bold & Brave: Ten Heroes Who Won Women the Right to Vote**

Gladwell, Malcolm. *The Tipping Point: How Little Things Can Make a Big Difference**

Goldin, Kara. *Undaunted: Overcoming Doubts and Doubters**

Gottlieb, Lori. *Maybe You Should Talk To Someone: A Therapist, Her Therapist, and Our Lives Revealed**

Halpern, Justin. *Sh*t My Dad Says*

Harris, Dan. *10% Happier: How I Tamed the Voice in My Head, Reduced Stress Without Losing My Edge, and Found Self-Help That Actually Works—A True Story*

Hershberg, Rebecca Schrag. *The Tantrum Survival Guide: Tune In to Your Toddler's Mind (and Your Own) to Calm the Craziness and Make Family Fun Again**

Hesser, Amanda. *Cooking for Mr. Latte: A Food Lover's Courtship, with Recipes*

Jackson, Laura Lynne. *Signs: The Secret Language of the Universe**

Krakauer, Jon. *Into Thin Air: A Personal Account of the Mt. Everest Disaster*

Krementz, Jill. *A Very Young Dancer*

Kübler-Ross, Elisabeth and David Kessler. *On Grief and Grieving: Finding the Meaning of Grief Through the Five Stages of Loss*

Lamott, Anne. *Bird by Bird: Some Instructions on Writing and Life**

Lopate, Phillip. *The Art of the Personal Essay: An Anthology from the Classical Era to the Present**

Mann, Jen. *I Just Want to Pee Alone**

Marx, Karl and Friedrich Engels. *The Communist Manifesto*

Mayle, Peter. *French Lessons: Adventures with Knife, Fork, and Corkscrew*

McCraw, Thomas K. *Creating Modern Capitalism: How Entrepreneurs, Companies, and Countries Triumphed in Three Industrial Revolutions*

Mogel, Wendy. *The Blessing of a Skinned Knee: Using Jewish Teachings to Raise Self-Reliant Children*

Monaghan, Annabel. *Does This Volvo Make My Butt Look Big? Thoughts for Moms and Other Tired People**

Murkoff, Heidi. *What to Expect When You're Expecting*

New York Times. *Portraits: 9/11/01: The Collected "Portraits of Grief" from The New York Times*

Ogilvy, David. *Ogilvy on Advertising*

Okun, Stacey. *Town & Country Elegant Weddings*

Owens, Zibby. *Moms Don't Have Time To: A Quarantine Anthology; Moms Don't Have Time to Have Kids: A Timeless Anthology**

Phelan, Thomas W. *1-2-3 Magic: The New 3-Step Discipline for Calm, Effective, and Happy Parenting*

Quindlen, Anna. *Living Out Loud**; *Nanaville: Adventures in Grandparenting**

Robbins, Alexandra and Abby Wilner. *Quarterlife Crisis: The Unique Challenges of Life in Your Twenties*

Rodsky, Eve. *Find Your Unicorn Space: Reclaim Your Creative Life in a Too-Busy World**

Rubin, Gretchen. *The Happiness Project: Or, Why I Spent a Year Trying to Sing in the Morning, Clean My Closets, Fight Right, Read Aristotle, and Generally Have More Fun**

Sacks, Oliver. *Awakenings*

Sandberg, Sheryl. *Lean In: Women, Work, and the Will to Lead*

Schultz, Howard. *Pour Your Heart into It: How Starbucks Built a Company One Cup at a Time*

Schwarzman, Stephen A. *What It Takes: Lessons in the Pursuit of Excellence**

Sedaris, David. *Me Talk Pretty One Day**

Sincero, Jen. *You Are a Badass: How to Stop Doubting Your Greatness and Start Living an Awesome Life**

Smokler, Jill. *Motherhood Comes Naturally (and Other Vicious Lies)*

Sorkin, Andrew Ross. *Too Big to Fail: The Inside Story of How Wall Street and Washington Fought to Save the Financial System—and Themselves*

Underhill, Paco. *Why We Buy: The Science of Shopping*

Wilder-Taylor, Stefanie. *Sippy Cups Are Not for Chardonnay: And Other Things I Had to Learn as a New Mom*

Yale Daily News Staff. *The Insider's Guide to the Colleges: 1999*

BIOGRAPHY/MEMOIR

Agassi, Andre. *Open: An Autobiography**

Albom, Mitch. *Finding Chika: A Little Girl, an Earthquake, and the Making of a Family*; *Tuesdays with Morrie: An Old Man, a Young Man, and Life's Greatest Lesson**

Armstrong, Heather. *It Sucked and Then I Cried: How I Had a Baby, a Breakdown, and a Much Needed Margarita*

Biden, Jill. *Where the Light Enters: Building a Family, Discovering Myself**

Burton, Susan. *Empty: A Memoir**

Cheever, Susan. *Note Found in a Bottle: My Life as a Drinker*

Cheney, Terri. *Modern Madness: An Owner's Manual**

Clegg, Bill. *Portrait of an Addict as a Young Man: A Memoir**

Corrigan, Kelly. *The Middle Place**

Crystal, Billy. *700 Sundays*

Danler, Stephanie. *Stray: A Memoir**

Dederer, Claire. *Poser: My Life in Twenty-three Yoga Poses**

DeGeneres, Ellen. *Seriously . . . I'm Kidding*

Didion, Joan. *The Year of Magical Thinking*

Dunham, Lena. *Not That Kind of Girl: A Young Woman Tells You What She's "Learned"**

Evans, Sara. *Born to Fly: A Memoir**

Fey, Tina. *Bossypants*

Frey, James. *My Friend Leonard**

Gideon, Melanie. *The Slippery Year: A Meditation on Happily Ever After**

Gould, Melissa. *Widowish: A Memoir**

Hager, Jenna Bush. *Everything Beautiful in Its Time: Seasons of Love and Loss**

Haney, Lynn. *Chris Evert, the Young Champion*

Hillenbrand, Laura. *Seabiscuit: An American Legend*

Karr, Mary. *Lit: A Memoir*

Kaysen, Susanna. *Girl, Interrupted*

Keys, Alicia. *More Myself: A Journey**

King, Stephen. *On Writing: A Memoir of the Craft*

Knapp, Caroline. *Drinking: A Love Story*

Knight, Phil. *Shoe Dog: A Memoir by the Creator of Nike*

Kogan, Deborah Copaken. *Shutterbabe: Adventures in Love and War**

Lawrence, Mary Wells. *A Big Life (in Advertising)*

Lewis, Michael. *Liar's Poker*

Lyons, Dan. *Disrupted: My Misadventure in the Start-Up Bubble*

Maslin, Abby. *Love You Hard: A Memoir of Marriage, Brain Injury, and Reinventing Love**

McColl, Sarah. *Joy Enough**

McCourt, Frank. *Angela's Ashes*

McInerny, Nora. *No Happy Endings**

Merkin, Daphne. *This Close to Happy: A Reckoning with Depression**

Nafisi, Azar. *Reading Lolita in Tehran: A Memoir in Books*

Newman, Leigh. *Still Points North: One Alaskan Childhood, One Grown-up World, One Long Journey Home**

Pataki, Allison. *Beauty in the Broken Places: A Memoir of Love, Faith, and Resilience**

Patchett, Ann. *Truth & Beauty: A Friendship**

Pausch, Randy and Jeffrey Zaslow. *The Last Lecture*

Plymale, Stephanie Thornton. *American Daughter: A Memoir of Intergenerational Trauma, a Mother's Dark Secrets, and a Daughter's Quest for Redemption**

Powell, Julie. *Julie & Julia: 365 Days, 524 Recipes, 1 Tiny Apartment*

Rakoff, Joanna. *My Salinger Year**

Schwalbe, Will. *The End of Your Life Book Club**

Shapiro, Dani. *Hourglass: Time, Memory, Marriage; Inheritance: A Memoir of Genealogy, Paternity, and Love; Slow Motion: A Memoir of a Life Rescued by Tragedy**

Shapiro, Susan. *Five Men Who Broke My Heart*; *Lighting Up: How I Stopped Smoking, Drinking, and Everything Else I Loved in Life Except Sex**

Smith, Claire Bidwell. *The Rules of Inheritance**

Solomon, Andrew. *The Noonday Demon: An Atlas of Depression*

Strayed, Cheryl. *Wild: From Lost to Found on the Pacific Crest Trail**

Streeter, Leslie Gray. *Black Widow: A Sad-Funny Journey Through Grief for People Who Normally Avoid Books with Words Like "Journey" in the Title**

Turow, Scott. *One L: The Turbulent True Story of a First Year at Harvard Law School*

Waldman, Ayelet. *Bad Mother: A Chronicle of Maternal Crimes, Minor Calamities, and Occasional Moments of Grace*

Walls, Jeannette. *The Glass Castle*

Weiss, Piper. *You All Grow Up and Leave Me: A Memoir of Teenage Obsession**

COOKBOOKS

Garten, Ina. *The Barefoot Contessa Cookbook*

Paltrow, Gwyneth. *It's All Easy: Delicious Weekday Recipes for the Super-Busy Home Cook*

Seinfeld, Jessica. *Deceptively Delicious: Simple Secrets to Get Your Kids Eating Good Food*

Turshen, Julia. *Simply Julia: 110 Easy Recipes for Healthy Comfort Food**

POETRY

Kenney, John. *Love Poems for Married People**; *Love Poems for People with Children**

Whitman, Walt. *Leaves of Grass*

CHILDREN'S FICTION/YA

Blume, Judy. *Are You There God? It's Me, Margaret*

Carroll, Lewis. *Alice's Adventures in Wonderland*

Daughtry, Mikki and Rachael Lippincott. *All This Time**

Jaques, Faith. *Tilly's Rescue*

Jeffers, Oliver. *How to Catch a Star**

Lilly, Evangeline. *The Squickerwonkers**

Mlynowski, Sarah. *Fairest of All* (Whatever After #1)*; *Upside-Down Magic**

Oneal, Zibby. *The Language of Goldfish*

Owens, Zibby. *Princess Charming**

Pascal, Francine. *Best Friends* (Sweet Valley Twins)

Portman, Natalie. *Natalie Portman's Fables**

Townsend, Sue. *The Secret Diary of Adrian Mole, Aged 13 ¾*

White, E. B. *Charlotte's Web*

Willems, Mo. *We Are in a Book!* (An Elephant & Piggie Book)

ABOUT THE AUTHOR

Photo © 2021 Kyle Owens

Zibby Owens is the creator and host of the award-winning podcast *Moms Don't Have Time to Read Books*. Zibby, named "New York's Most Powerful Book-fluencer" by *New York* magazine's Vulture, conducts warm, inquisitive conversations with authors, making her daily show a top literary podcast as selected by Oprah.com in 2019 and 2020. Zibby is the cofounder and CEO of Zibby Books, a publishing home for fiction and memoir. She's also the CEO of Moms Don't Have Time To, a media company that includes the Zcast podcast network, the Zibby Awards, *Moms Don't Have Time to Write* on Medium, Moms Don't Have Time to Grieve, and Moms Don't Have Time to Lose Weight on Instagram, Zibby's Virtual Book Club, and two anthologies, *Moms Don't Have Time To: A Quarantine Anthology* and *Moms Don't Have Time to Have Kids: A Timeless Anthology*. A regular contributor to *Good Morning America* and Katie Couric Media, Zibby has also contributed to the *Washington Post*, *Real Simple*, *Parents*, *Marie Claire*, *Slate*, and many other publications. She has appeared on *Good Morning America*, *CBS This Morning*, the BBC, and other news outlets. Her first children's book, *Princess Charming*, will soon be followed by a second. A graduate of Yale University and Harvard Business School, Zibby currently lives in New York with her husband, Kyle Owens of Morning Moon Productions, and four children ages seven to fourteen. She always has a book nearby. For more information, visit www.zibbyowens.com and follow her on Instagram @zibbyowens. Just don't ask her how she does it all; she has no clue.

Visit www.bookendsmemoir.com for more.